# URBAN CATHOLICS

*Urban Catholicism in England and Wales*
*from 1829 to the present day*

# Urban Catholics

*Urban Catholicism in England and Wales*
*from 1829 to the present day*

JOHN HICKEY
B.A., Dip.Ed., M.A.

THE CATHOLIC BOOK CLUB
121 CHARING CROSS ROAD
LONDON W.C. 2

Geoffrey Chapman Ltd
18 High Street, Wimbledon, London SW 19

Geoffrey Chapman (Ireland) Ltd
5–7 Main Street, Blackrock, County Dublin

Geoffrey Chapman Pty Ltd
459 Little Collins Street, Melbourne, Australia

*First published 1967*

*This book is set in 11/13 Point Imprint*

Printed in Great Britain by Compton Printing Ltd.,
London and Aylesbury

# Contents

# Contents

# 1. Introduction: Scope of the Study

The aim of this work is to attempt an analysis of the development of social relationships between urban Catholic groups in England and Wales and their neighbours since the establishment, in its present form, of Catholicism in the early nineteenth century.

There is now developing in England an increasing awareness among Catholic as well as other scholars, of the need for scientific study of the pattern of Catholic life in a modern urban, industrial environment. There is a need, as well, to provide a perspective in which one aspect of this work—the problem of social relationships between Catholics and non-Catholics—could be set. To provide such a perspective account has to be taken of origins and of the developments through which the urban Catholic groups have passed since their formation in the first half of the nineteenth century; and a portion of this study is devoted to such an account.

There have been several studies of racial minorities in Britain which have proved very useful for identifying the social factors which affect the relationships between members of such minorities and society in general. Our understanding of the pattern of life of immigrant groups and of the forces which act for or against their assimilation into their social environment has been greatly increased by the work of scholars like M. Banton (*The Coloured Quarter*, London, 1955), S. Collins (*Coloured Minorities in Britain*, London, 1951) and K. Little (*Negroes in Britain*, London, 1948). There has also been one study of a religious minority in this country which has been of considerable value for the present work. M. Freedman in his book *A Minority in Britain* (London, 1957) has set out a pattern of the development of the Jewish settlement over a period of time. He has also put forward an analysis of the means by which

its members have come to terms with their social environment and
established for themselves an identifiable position in the larger
society outside that of their co-religionists.

There has been no such study of Catholics in England and
Wales. In order to find work on Catholics which could be used to
compare and contrast their progress from an underprivileged and
isolated minority and to use as a guide to an analysis of the development of their relationships with the remainder of society, it has
been necessary to look to America. There a continuing debate is in
process—involving a number of Catholic sociologists and historians
—on various aspects of Catholic life and achievement as compared
with that of their non-Catholic fellow Americans.[1] The most
illuminating study, however, from the point of view of this essay, is
that undertaken by W. Herberg and published under the title
*Protestant, Catholic, Jew* (New York, 1955). Herberg develops a
thesis which shows that the history of the assimilation of American
Catholic groups followed an identifiable pattern. This pattern
contains a recognisable series of stages through which the
immigrants and their descendants passed from a state of isolation
to one in which they were able to be assimilated into American
society on terms which did not involve a complete loss of their
identity.

The present study is both historical and sociological. The
historical aspects of the work are contained mainly in the first
three sections and are of considerable importance in putting the
present situation of Catholics in urban England and Wales in their
proper context. Some aspects of English Catholicism have their
roots far back in pre-Reformation times, but a substantial element
of the Catholic Church in England is of very recent origin and
owes little to English tradition. Thus, when the term 'English
Catholic' is used a careful distinction must be made between the
different 'types' of Catholic who live in England and who together
constitute the Catholic Church.

[1] See, for example: Tracy Ellis, 'American Catholics and the Intellectual Life',
Putz, L. J. (ed.) *The Catholic Church*, U.S.A. (Chicago, 1956); O'Dea, Thomas,
*The American Catholic Dilemma* (New York, 1958); Donovan, J. D., *The
Academic Man in the Catholic College* (New York, 1964); Greeley, A., *Religion
and Career. A study of college graduates* (New York, 1963).

With these considerations in mind, the historical section of the study has been devised so as to give some indication of the development of Catholicism in England and Wales from the beginning of the nineteenth century until the present time. Within this framework reference will be made to the different elements, including the old English Catholics whose families had maintained the Faith intact since pre-Reformation days, the converts, who entered the Church at different times in the nineteenth century, and the immigrant Irish who constituted the vast majority of the Catholics who lived in the British Isles.

It is not possible in a study of this sort to give a detailed account of the history of these groups of Catholics. The story of Catholics in Britain from the Reformation to the end of the eighteenth century is still slowly being written. Attempts have been made in the past to write a complete history of English Catholicism in this period but these efforts, for the most part, have not been entirely satisfactory, largely because there has been insufficient evidence available on which to base reliable historical judgements. The situation is changing considerably for the better as the result of the devoted efforts of a number of scholars working in the field of recusant studies.[1] A number of localities in England and Wales have been intensively studied and the fruit of this research, though still relatively inaccessible, embedded, as it often is, in unpublished theses and individual articles in a variety of learned journals, have gone a long way towards altering considerably previous judgements on the English Catholicism of the sixteenth, seventeenth and eighteenth centuries. A definitive work, gathering together the fruits of these scholarly labours, still waits to be written, but in 1961 Miss M. D. R. Leys—one of the most prominent English recusant historians—published her book, *Catholics in England, 1559–1829* (London, 1961). This work, in Miss Leys' own words, is 'an attempt to examine the relations that existed between the Catholics in England and their neighbours during the years when the exercise of their faith was banned by the law', and I have drawn on it for some of the short section of this study which deals

---

[1] For example, the work of Dom Hugh Aveling (North England), J. A. Williams (West Country), and F. Pugh and J. M. Cleary (Wales).

with the position of Catholics in England at the end of the eighteenth and the beginning of the nineteenth centuries.

The sociological aspect of this work is an attempt to draw a coherent picture of the process of assimilation of urban Catholics in England and Wales into the larger society in which their settlements were established. This has involved an analysis of the social and religious factors which encourage or discourage assimilation and the study has been planned to make this analysis as clear as possible. Thus in Section 4 those factors making for the isolation of the immigrant settlements, which were found to be common to a number of urban areas in different and widely separated parts of England and Wales, have been outlined. This is followed in Section 5A and 5B by a study of one urban Catholic community in order to bring out clearly the manner in which these factors operated. Section 6 has been inserted at that particular stage of the study in order to show how one particular, and very important aspect of their historical development affected the relationships between Catholics and their neighbours.

In the last section of the book an attempt is made to assess the present position of urban Catholics in England and Wales as far as relationships with their neighbours are concerned. This assessment is made in the light of the work of the sociologists already mentioned, with particular reference to Herberg's thesis that an immigrant, religious, minority group passes through three stages— isolation, a period of adaptation when this separation is breaking down, and assimilation into a recognisable status in the larger society. Differences between the situations of immigrant Catholics in England and America are brought out and it is estimated that in England Catholics have progressed no further than the second stage. The last part of Section 7 includes an examination of some areas in which future research could profitably be done.

It has been indicated throughout the work where material collected and published by other researchers has been used. The remainder, which constitutes the bulk of the material and the whole of the analysis, is the sole responsibility of the author.

## 2. Background: Religious, Social, Political

OUTLINE OF THE PHYSICAL GROWTH AND DISTRIBUTION OF THE
CATHOLIC POPULATION TO 1961

The statistics which are available and accessible show the outlines of the growth of the Catholic Church in England and Wales from the beginning of the nineteenth century until the middle of the twentieth century. Until recently it has been extremely difficult to obtain reliable data about the size and distribution of the Catholic population in England and Wales. There was no single official source of information on this point as the government censuses, carried out at ten-yearly intervals since 1811, contained, and contain, no question on the religious adherence of individuals. An attempt was made, in 1851, to arrive at some measure of the religious affiliation of the population, when H. Mann was asked to conduct an enquiry into Church attendance. His voluminous report on *Religious Worship in England and Wales* (London, 1854), is a mine of information about one aspect of religious affiliation— religious 'practice', defined as attendance at Church—but it suffers from the inherent drawbacks of a survey conducted on one particular day as opposed to an enquiry based on extended observation.

The lack of reliable official sources means that recourse must be had to unofficial contemporary estimates in order to gain some idea of the size of the Catholic population. These estimates vary a great deal, and no real reliance can be put upon them; they serve merely to give some indication of the number of Catholics in England and Wales at varying periods. In 1780 it was estimated that there were 56,500 Catholics in England and Wales.[1] In 1829, after the passing

[1] Jos Berrington: Quoted by A. E. C. W. Spencer in an unpublished paper entitled 'The Demography and Sociography of the Catholic Community of England and Wales', 1965 (Downside Symposium).

11

of the Emancipation Act, which finally revoked the most burden-
some penal legislation of the three previous centuries and put
Catholics on an equal footing with other citizens of their social
class, it was rumoured that there were two million Catholics in
England and Wales.[1] This estimate seems highly unlikely, even
considering the increasing number of Irish immigrants who were
entering the country, and could well have been the product of the
alarmist propaganda that was being disseminated at this time in
Protestant Britain, many of whose most substantial citizens looked
with fear on the prospect of a restoration of popery.[2]

In 1840, the *Catholic Directory*, while repeating the figure of two
million in an editorial, gives the actual size of the Catholic population as 700,000. If we take this figure in conjunction with the
census of 1851, which gives a total of 519,959 Irish-born perstons
in England and Wales—a proportion of whom came from Protesant
Ireland—we may roughly estimate that in the middle of the nineteenth century there was a Catholic population of between 700,000
and 800,000. By 1886 the estimate in the *Catholic Directory* had
risen to around 1,500,000 and this figure was repeated untli 1903.
The next published figures do not appear until the 1912 edition of
the *Catholic Directory* when the Catholic population was estimated
at 1,710,000.

In 1951 the official estimate given in the *Catholic Directory* was
2,837,000. It is at this stage that the work of A. E. C. W. Spencer,
formerly Director of the Newman Demographic Survey and now
Head of the Department of Socio-Religious Research at Cavendish
Square College, London, begins to throw a much more revealing
light on the real size of the Catholic population of England and
Wales. The Newman Demographic Survey estimate for 1951 indicated a Catholic population in England and Wales of 4·67 million.[3]
This figure had risen to 5·6 million by 1961, a total that has been
largely confirmed by the results of market research and public
opinion samples.[4]

---

[1] See A. E. C. W. Spencer *ibid.* Figures taken from *The Catholic Magazine*,
1834 and *Blackwood's Magazine*, vol. 44, no. 276, October, 1838.
[2] See below.
[3] See A. E. C. W. Spencer, *ibid.*
[4] *Ibid.*

Briefly, then, the Catholic population of England and Wales has risen from approximately 50,000 in the last decades of the eighteenth century, to about 7 or 800,000 by the middle of the nineteenth century. This figure had increased to something in the region of 1·5 million at the start of the twentieth century, and the most reliable contemporary estimates indicate a figure of 5·5 million Catholics in England and Wales at the present time.

The next logical question to be answered is how these Catholics were distributed throughout the country. For the period at the end of the eighteenth century there is only the evidence of the witness quoted previously; he estimated that out of the total of 56,000 Catholics, 25,000 were in the London Area, and of those, 20,000 lived in London itself. In the North of England it was also estimated that a high proportion of the Catholics lived in industrial

*Table 1:* Total population and Catholic population of main cities and counties, 1961.[1]

| City (1) | Total populat. (000's) | Catholic populat. (000's) | % Catholic | Admin. county (2) | Total populat. (000's) | Catholic populat. (000's) | % Catholic |
|---|---|---|---|---|---|---|---|
| London | 3,195 | 135 | 23·0 | Middlesex | 2,230 | 300 | 13·4 |
| Birmingham | 1,106 | 217 | 19·6 | Lancashire | 2,207 | 450 | 20·4 |
| Liverpool | 747 | 310 | 41·5 | Essex | 1,859 | 138 | 1·4 |
| Manchester | 661 | 210 | 31·7 | Kent | 1,671 | 114 | 6·8 |
| Leeds | 511 | 78 | 15·2 | Yorkshire, | | | |
| Sheffield | 494 | 38·5 | 7·8 | W.R. | 1,649 | 110 | 6·7 |
| Bristol | 436 | 41 | 9·4 | Surrey | 1,481 | 138 | 9·3 |
| Nottingham | 312 | 26·5 | 8·5 | Staffordshire | 985 | 62 | 6·3 |
| Coventry | 305 | 65 | 21·3 | Durham | 953 | 141 | 14·8 |
| Kingston- | | | | Cheshire | 921 | 84 | 9·1 |
| upon-Hull | 303 | 24·5 | 8·1 | Hertfordshire | 832 | 80 | 9·6 |
| Bradford | 296 | 51 | 17·2 | Hampshire | 762 | 48·5 | 6·4 |
| Leicester | 273 | 26·5 | 9·7 | Glamorgan | 746 | 41 | 5·5 |
| Newcastle | | | | Derbyshire | 745 | 32·5 | 4·4 |
| upon-Tyne | 269 | 53 | 10·9 | Warwickshire | 613 | 47 | 1·7 |
| Stoke-on- | | | | Nottingham- | | | |
| Trent | 266 | 29 | 10·9 | shire | 591 | 30 | 5·7 |
| Cardiff | 256 | 49 | 19·2 | Devonshire | 538 | 20 | 3·7 |
| Croydon | 252 | 26 | 10·3 | Somerset | 518 | 21·5 | 4·1 |

(1) London and all county boroughs with populations exceeding 250,000.
(2) All administrative counties with populations exceeding 500,000.

[1] A. E. C. W. Spencer, *ibid.*

towns. This pattern of the bulk of Catholics being concentrated in the big towns and forming urban groups was continued throughout the nineteenth century and into the twentieth.[1] The census figures since 1811, which give the birth place of each citizen, indicate that almost all the Irish-born population lived in the big towns—a fact which is not surprising when it is considered that the main reason compelling the Irish to leave their homes was the desire to find work to provide then with a fairly regular means of subsistence.[2] It was natural that they should flock to the new industrial towns and form the nucleus of urban Catholicism in England and Wales.

The above table indicates the distribution of Catholics in 1961.

DIVISIONS AMONGST CATHOLICS

It is necessary now to look beyond the mere figures of the size of the Catholic population and to attempt an analysis of some of its main divisions. 'Divisions' is an appropriate term to use in this context because there are, in fact, at least three main sectors of English Catholicism and the separation and isolation of each one from the other is of great significance for the sociological analysis of the later section of this work.

The three groups involved can be identified in the following way. First of all, the 'old Catholics', defined as those Catholics living in England who retained their faith throughout the period of the Reformation and the intervening centuries before the nineteenth century. This group, a more detailed description of which follows below, was small and exclusive in character. The second group consists of the converts of the nineteenth and twentieth century. Again, these are few in number but include amongst them men like Cardinal Newman and Cardinal Manning whose conversion was of great significance for the Church in England. The third

---

[1] See for a comprehensive survey of emigration to England of Irish Catholics from 1841 to 1951: *Commission on Emigration and other Population Problems: 1948–1954 Reports (Dublin)*. See also: *Irish Trade Journal and Statistical Bulletin*, June, 1955 (Dublin), Stationery Office and Central Statistics Office.

[2] *Census of Great Britain*. Volumes published at ten yearly intervals (with the exception of 1941) since 1811.

group consisted of by far the largest number of Catholics in England and Wales—the urban group who were mainly Irish in origin and whose contact with the two other sections of English Catholicism was in any real sense, negligible. This third group will be examined in detail in the main body of the study.

I have not attempted to give a factual account of the physical development of the Church in the nineteenth and twentieth centuries. There are no details included here of church-building, foundation of religious communities, development of schools and colleges, except in so far as they were necessary for the development of the analysis that has been undertaken. The straightforward narrative of all these events is already available from a number of sources, which are given in the Bibliography and which are easily accessible. These sources have been used to provide a background to this study and I have indicated throughout the text the origin of my information.

I have concentrated on the aspect which is most pertinent to this study, i.e. the relationship between Catholics and their neighbours of the same social class and background during the period with which we are concerned. The bulk of the material—the body of the thesis—will concern that particular group of 'urban' Catholics who were Irish in origin and depressed in social class, but the other two groups of Catholics must be dealt with briefly first of all.

## (i) *Old Catholics*

For the two centuries prior to 1788, Catholics in England had been burdened with a penal code which, among other things, had branded priests as traitors and imposed ruinously high financial penalties for recusancy—non-attendance at the services of the Established Church. In 1699 an Act had been passed which made Catholics who became priests or schoolmasters subject to life imprisonment and which promised rewards to those who secured their conviction. Papists were also prohibited from inheriting or purchasing land.

The penal code had never been systematically applied in its full rigour against Catholics in England; the severity of its punishments and its manifest injustices when it came to individual cases, made their neighbours unwilling to inform on many Catholics, and judges reluctant to operate the law in the cases which were brought before them. This at least was true of the eighteenth century when there was a noticeable slackening in government measures against Catholics and when Catholics themselves were coming closer to their neighbours. Generally there was an atmosphere of religious tolerance and a sense that penal laws were a disgrace to the statute book.

For their part, the English papists were anxious both to rid themselves of the heavy restrictions which the law placed upon their activities—even if it did not, in practice, threaten their lives—and to demonstrate publicly their devotion to the monarchy and their loyalty to the English government. They were weary of being cramped in their business and professional lives and they resented bitterly the accusation of disloyalty or lack of patriotism. These considerations applied particularly to Catholic lawyers and wealthy landowners. The former were only able to act as conveyancers, all other branches of legal activity being closed to them, and the latter suffered acutely from the Act of 1699 which forced them to adopt all sorts of subterfuges whenever they bought or inherited land. A group of these laymen, led by a lawyer called Sheldon, accordingly petitioned the King; the petition was so well-received that a Bill was drafted to secure the repeal of the Act of 1699 and the Roman Catholic Relief Act was passed in 1778. The main beneficiaries of this Act were the landowners, for the earlier penal laws were retained and priests were still officially traitors. The Act gave relief only to those who took an oath of loyalty to the crown and, as a result, Catholic laymen and priests came forward rapidly to take this oath. From this time on, prayers for the King were said in every Catholic chapel in the country and Catholics were officially recognised as loyal Englishmen.

The process of removing the penal legislation took a great step forward in 1829 when Catholics were given political rights. Distinctions were still made, however, between Catholics and their fellow citizens. The former were now given the vote—within the narrow limits of the existing franchise—and were entitled to be elected to the House of Commons or to sit in the House of

Lords. They could not, however, hold the offices of Lord
Chancellor, Lord Keeper or Lord Lieutenant of Ireland; all other
offices in local or national government were open to them. Catholics
were forbidden to take part in any election to any body connected
with the Church of England; this seems scarcely relevant as a
prohibition until it is realised that it extended to all organisations
which were held to be an integral part of the ecclesiastical system
and this included the universities. Recruitment to religious orders,
including the Jesuits, was forbidden and members of these orders
had to be specially registered. Finally, Catholics in political life had
to take an oath 'not to disturb or weaken the protestant religion'
and to deny that the Pope had any political rights in England.

During the remainder of the nineteenth century the last restrictions against Catholics were removed but it was not until 1926 that
the last traces of penal legislation disappeared from the statute
book, and a Catholic is still unable to hold the office of Lord
Chancellor.

In the nineteenth century, the 'old Catholics', the descendants of
those who had endured the penal period between the Reformation
and the sixteenth century, were mainly to be found outside the
towns.[1] The heaviest concentration of estates where the owners,
tenants, farmers and labourers had remained Catholics was in the
north of England, in Northumberland, Durham, Lancashire and
Yorkshire. In the Midlands, a smaller proportion of Catholics in
the same social class and with the same occupation existed, while
in East Anglia, the south and south-west of England, and Wales,
Catholics were few, and scattered.

Within the limitations of the restrictions laid upon them, these
Catholics lived a life very similar to that of their fellow-Englishmen
of the same social class. Those who belonged to the ranks of the
squirearchy were absorbed in the routine of rural life. The sons of
the squire lived on the family estates and when those estates were
large—as in the case of the wealthier landed proprietors—they

[1] For a discussion of the 'old Catholics' in England in the 19th century see
David Mathew 'Old Catholics and Converts' in *The English Catholics, 1850–1950*,
ed., G. A. Beck, (London, 1950). See also: David Mathew *Catholicism in England*
(London, 1936). I am indebted to this author for much of the material contained
in the paragraphs on the 'old Catholics'.

were often managed by relatives of the owner. Deep-rooted traditions of rural living were established among this class, strengthened by extended ties of kinship and by bonds of neighbourship with the Protestant squires and great landowners.

This group of Catholics were little affected by the beginnings of industrialism. The industrial areas of Lancashire, in particular the towns of Preston, Liverpool and Chorley, attracted some of the younger tenants and labourers on the Catholic estates so that the urban Catholic communities in these areas numbered English as well as Irish Catholics amongst them. The old Catholics, however, did not benefit as much as other sections of the community from the new industrial prosperity. There had always been Catholics among the more prosperous merchants, in the legal and medical professions and in trades like printing. In the new, rising class of wealthy industrialists, the mill, mine and factory-owners— Catholics were few and far between so that in the new industrial towns Catholics were to be found almost exclusively in the ranks of the workers and wage-earners.

At the same time, there is not much evidence to show that the old Catholics were of much account in the class of new investors; the squires, it seems, were conservative when it came to money matters and preferred to put their money into house property or land. Investment was not the only sphere which they neglected. There were whole areas of English life which, for one reason or another, Catholics did not penetrate, though there might be the occasional incursion of an isolated individual. These areas included the clerical and the academic worlds, the new industries and the groups generally from which the civil service was recruited. They did not exercise, either, any influence in the commercial and banking worlds, represented by the City of London. Until well into the nineteenth century it was the landed interest, and that alone, which was predominant amongst the old Catholics.

It is worthwhile from the point of view of this study to look briefly at the activities of these representatives of Catholicism. The peers amongst them, approximately twenty in number in the middle of the nineteenth century, including those who held Scottish and Irish titles, were not notably active in political circles. Indeed between them they had only twelve votes in the House of Lords and, even if they had wanted to, could not have exercised any significant influence as a group.[1] It seems that a pattern of living had emerged amongst the wealthier Catholics in which they settled comfortably into a well-ordered rural existence, removed from contact with the new political, industrial and social developments which were causing such strife and upheaval in England in the nineteenth century. They were able to live what was practically a self-contained life; each Catholic estate of any size had its own chapel and each great family had its own chaplain, often a regular clergyman. It would be too much to say that they were markedly reactionary in their approach to the problems of the nineteenth century; it would, it seems, be more correct to describe their attitude as one of detachment and, to a large extent, disinterest. They were as generous as they could be in their efforts to help the spiritual welfare of the new, poor Catholics, crowded into the towns; they provided them with chapels, where possible and appropriate, and donated to private charity, but they did all this without in any way understanding the real and pressing needs or problems of the new urban communities.

Their attitude towards converts showed a similar disinclination to emerge from the old ways. Converts were acceptable, and accepted, provided they, in turn, were prepared to accept in full the general way of life of those who had maintained their faith through the penal times. A convert was judged by his willingness 'to enter within the citadel'.[2] It is not easy to say, immediately, why the Catholics who could possibly have provided leadership in many spheres for their main body of co-religionists in the towns, chose instead to lead relatively secluded lives. Had the long years of existing as a politically under-privileged minority established a tradition of exclusiveness which was now too deeply entrenched to be destroyed? This seems an over-simplified—though neat and tidy—explanation when we consider that, as has been mentioned

[1] See Mathew 'Old Catholics and Converts' (*The English Catholics, op. cit.*). In his work *Catholicism in England*, Archbishop Mathew gives details of those exceptional Catholics of this class who *did* play some part in politics. (See also Section 4 below.)

[2] Mathew, 'Old Catholics and Converts', *op. cit.*

earlier, relationships between Catholics and their Protestant neighbours had been improving at least since the first decades of the
eighteenth century. Other factors must come under consideration
and some of them will be examined at the end of this section.

## (ii) *Converts*

The second, and smallest, group to be considered are the
nineteenth-century converts to Catholicism. It is misleading to
describe these as a 'group' if by this we mean a homogeneous
body of people with easily definable characteristics. In fact, it is
very difficult to describe them at all unless we restrict ourselves
to isolating personalities and the one movement which began
within the Established Church and concluded one phase of its
life with several of its most prominent members leaving this
Church to become Catholics. We refer here, of course, to the
Oxford Movement, which began as an attempt by a group of
scholars, centred upon Oxford, to defend the Anglican Church
against what they considered to be the menace of Liberalism.[1]
These men conceived their task as being to re-state as clearly and
firmly as possible the dogmas upon which the Anglican Church
was founded; they were concerned at the inroads being made into
tradition and belief by people who were content to interpret ancient
teachings—some of them of fundamental importance for the basis
of the Anglican belief—vaguely and loosely. They felt that the
spiritual authority of the Anglican Church was being undermined
and the magisterium of its bishops whittled away.[2]

[1] There have been a great many books written on the Oxford Movement and a
number of them are listed in the Bibliography. Perhaps the most moving and, in
some ways, illuminating account of the Movement by one who was closely connected with its leading personalities is to be found in the work of Dean Church.
See R. W. Church. *The Oxford Movement, 1833-45* (London, 1891).

[2] J. H. Newman. *Apologia Pro Vita Sua* (London, 1864). In this Newman
writes '. . . I felt affection for my own Church, but not tenderness; I felt dismay
at her prospects, anger and scorn at her do-nothing perplexity. I thought that if
Liberalism once got a footing within her, it was sure of the victory in the event.
I saw that Reformation principles were powerless to rescue her. As to leaving
her, the thought never crossed my imagination; still I ever kept before me that
there was something greater than the Established Church, and that that was the
Church Catholic and Apostolic, set up from the beginning, of which she was but
the local presence and organ.

In order to combat this they issued, largely under the direction of John Henry (later Cardinal) Newman, a series of pamphlets entitled 'Tracts for the Times'. These, though dealing with theological matters of profound importance, were written in as simple language as possible in order to give them a wide circulation. It is not necessary here to give the details of the history of the Tractarians; the whole Oxford Movement is well documented and books dealing with the life and influence of Cardinal Newman appear regularly. The point can be made, however, that the writings of Newman and his associates produced a profound impact on the Anglican Church, and the conversions which followed the Oxford Movement of men like Newman himself, Faber, Ward, Ambrose St John, Coffin, Dalgairns, etc. were of considerable importance for the Roman Catholic Church in England and Wales. For reasons which we will examine later, the real significance of the conversions which followed the Oxford Movement, both immediately and throughout the nineteenth century, for the Catholic Church in England, did not become apparent until very recently. The 'intelligent, well-educated laity' that Newman desired is ever more rapidly coming into being—the process of its formation receiving a boost from the Second Vatican Council and the continual re-assessment of the place of the laity in the Roman Catholic Church—and Newman's influence is probably more widespread now than at any time since his death.[1] The fact that the appearance of such a laity owes much to the operation of social factors outside the Church will, we hope, become clear later in this study.

She was nothing, unless she was this. She must be dealt with strongly, or she would be lost. There was need of a second Reformation' (Fontana edn., 1959, p. 119).

[1] The upsurge of interest in Newman in England, which is taking place now both inside and outside the Catholic Church, is evidenced by the growing popularity of 'Newman Studies'; see, for instance, the work of Fr. S. Dessain, who is in the process of editing Newman's letters and diaries, Miss Meriol Trevor, who has recently produced a two-volume life of Newman (see Bibliography) and J. Coulson, in whose latest work *Newman: A Portrait Restored* (London, 1965), can be found a complete guide to Newman's works.

## SOCIAL ISOLATION OF THESE GROUPS

The essential feature of these two groups—old Catholics and converts—from the point of view of the analysis of the development of urban Catholicism in England, is the extent to which they remained isolated from society in general and from each other in particular. Perhaps even more important is the degree to which they remained isolated from the third, and by far the largest group of Catholics in England, the Irish immigrants in the industrial towns. To discover the reasons for this situation one must take account of the political, social and religious factors which were operating at the time.

It is ironic that the date 1778 which marks, in many ways, the first step towards re-admittance of Catholics in England to full citizenship should also mark the beginning of a new period of isolation from their fellow Englishmen who were not Catholics. We are nowadays familiar with situations where the granting of concessions to an under-privileged group has destroyed the old relationship that existed between donor and recipient. The former is prepared to tolerate a situation in which the subordinate group, deprived, as it is, of any rights which would enable it to menace the security of the majority group, is allowed to live its own life without too much fear of intrusion. There is even the possibility of friendly and harmonious relationships between members of the different groups, and an atmosphere of peace and mutual good-will is created. This atmosphere is basically false because it is dependent entirely on the maintenance of the *status quo*, and that means a perpetuation of the situation where one of the groups is under-privileged. If the situation changes, if the minority are given some of the rights hitherto restricted to the majority, then elements within the majority will immediately see their own security threatened and will often respond violently to this threat—real or imagined. The false calm is shattered and the emergent minority suffers a sharp rebuff, relationships between the two groups become more strained than they had hitherto appeared, and the ensuing hostility guarantees the perpetuation and deepening of the gulf between them.

It was something of this nature which occurred after the Relief Act of 1778. We have seen that for a long time, in the eighteenth century the penal laws had not been rigorously enforced against Catholics and that the old Catholics had been growing closer to their non-Catholic neighbours. Edmund Burke, in 1780, described the penal laws as 'cruel outrages'; he believed that the English Reformation would not be complete until they were repealed.[1] He was particularly harsh in his denunciation of the Act of 1699 which, he said, 'condemned to beggary and to ignorance in their native land' the whole body of Catholics. The latter, he said, consisted 'mostly of our best manufacturers' and, if they had received no relief, would have been forced to emigrate to Flanders 'by the bigotry of a free country in an enlightened age'. But if the Catholics in England had as powerful an advocate as Burke to defend them, they had opponents who were even more powerful and, in the short run, more effective. The main opposition to 'popery' came not from the Anglican clergy but from the Protestant dissenters. The latter condemned anything which smacked of popery almost as venomously as had their Puritan forbears of the seventeenth century. Any concession to Roman Catholicism was, they felt, dangerous and evil; this view was so widespread that even John Wesley himself was able to speak, in 1780, of 'the purple power of Rome advancing by hasty strides to overspread this once more happy nation'.[2]

Wesley was not, however, responsible for beginning the violence which followed upon 1778. A Protestant association had been formed and, in November 1779, had elected as its president one Lord George Gordon. The latter was an eccentric character, verging in fact, on madness, but he was very effective as an agitator and his violent attacks on the Pope were well-received by the mass meetings at which they were delivered. Trouble first broke out in Scotland in 1779 following the introduction into Parliament of the Relief Bill for Scottish Catholics. Riots broke out in Edinburgh and other towns and Catholic chapels and the homes of individual Catholics were burned and plundered. While this was taking place —without any attempt on the part of the local authorities to stop

[1] For quotations from Edmund Burke see M. A. Leys, *op. cit.*
[2] Quoted by M. A. Leys, *op. cit.*

it—the General Assembly of the Church of Scotland issued a statement demanding that none of the penal laws against Catholics
should be repealed. In England, also the ground was being prepared for similar outbursts. Pamphlets were printed and sermons
were preached all demanding that no relief be given to papists.
Rumours were spread of the twenty-thousand Jesuits waiting in
Surrey to blow up the banks of the Thames and flood London, or
of the members of the same order who were plotting to assassinate
the King, George III. These rumours were calculated to inflame
the population, and led, almost inevitably it seems, to the events
of 1780.

On 4 January of that year a petition was presented by the
Protestant association to Parliament asking for the repeal of the
Act of 1778. The behaviour of Lord George Gordon in the House
of Commons was so peculiar, however, that neither he nor his
petition were taken seriously. Gordon then called a mass meeting
in London on 2 June; a very large crowd gathered, composed of
both religious fanatics and the riff-raff of the city, and the trouble
began. Catholics and those known to be their associates were
attacked and Catholic chapels were pillaged. The violence spread
wider and the disorder turned into very ugly rioting on a wide
scale; prisons were broken into, shops were looted and a distillery
was set on fire. There was much damage to property and many
people died. The mobs were not very discriminating in their choice
of victims for the Protestant Archbishop of York was assaulted as
well as a number of his fellow-bishops and many members of
Parliament. The violence went unchecked for a long time because
no magistrate dared to issue the proclamation which would enable
the troops to take action. It was not, in fact, until 8 June that the
King himself issued a proclamation and sent forces to restore order.
The troops were able to scatter the mobs quickly, but the casualties
among civilians were high; it was officially estimated that 285
people had been killed by the troops, but there were many more
who had died at the hands of the mobs themselves. Of the prisoners
who were taken, 21 were executed.

The effects of these Gordon riots upon Catholics in England can
be imagined. There had been no outbreak of persecution outside

London—the only incident being at Bath where a newly built Catholic chapel was destroyed—but Catholics were very alarmed. They had reason to be; they had observed the violent tone of the pamphlets distributed in 1779, they had heard the rumours—wild though they may have been—of Catholic plots to overthrow Protestantism and government and substitute the rule of the Pope, and they had heard a man of the calibre of John Wesley declaim against the purple power of Rome. Their Bishop—Challoner—had been forced to flee from the fury of a mob and their chapels in London had been pillaged and destroyed by their fellow townsmen. And all this had occurred as the result of an Act of Parliament which did little beyond acknowledge the fact that Catholics could be loyal citizens and were entitled to inherit and dispose of land. It is not, then, surprising if they felt discouraged from venturing forth from the comfortable seclusion of their estates and were inclined to turn back to a secure, if exclusive, way of life.

The opposition aroused in 1780 was confirmed and strengthened by the Act of 1829. As we have seen, the latter went considerably further than the Act of 1778 in granting concessions to the Catholic minority and thus made them even more of a potential menace in the eyes of sections of the majority. We shall see some of the manifestations of this opposition when we are considering the urban Catholics in later sections. It is sufficient to say here that the result of both acts was an increase in the social antagonism towards Catholicism so that it reached far greater proportions than in the penal days. The old relationship of apparent mutual respect and toleration disappeared with revocation of the laws which had made its existence possible, and the privileges of citizenship won by Catholics in the fifty years spanning the end of the eighteenth and the beginning of the nineteenth centuries were a contributory cause of the long separation from their neighbours which followed. This separation endured well into the present century and is only now showing signs of coming to an end.

To give point to the statements that have been made concerning the separation of the old Catholics from their fellow Englishmen of the same social class, we can make use of the testimony of an eye-witness. Newman, who describes the position of Catholics in

England in the nineteenth century, is a valuable witness for many reasons. Not only do the qualities of his mind and character make it difficult to challenge his judgements and testimony, but his life and educational and social background made him particularly qualified to speak of the old Catholics whose social status was similar to his own. Newman was born in 1801 and died in 1890, his life thus practically spans the nineteenth century; he was of the wealthy middle class and he was educated at a private school and at Oxford, being elected a Fellow of Oriel College in 1822.

In what is probably his best-known work, the *Apologia Pro Vita Sua*, Newman describes his arduous spiritual journey from Anglicanism to Roman Catholicism. At the same time, although his book is not in any way an 'autobiography' in the accepted sense, he does give revealing glimpses of the attitudes of himself and his contemporaries to Roman Catholics. In the following extract Newman describes Roman Catholics and Roman Catholicism, as he had seen them when still a schoolboy.

'Of course I must have got this practice [of "crossing" himself— a peculiarly Catholic custom] from some external source or other; but I can make no sort of conjecture whence: and certainly no one had even spoken to me on the subject of the Catholic Religion, which I only knew by name. The French master was an émigré Priest, but he was simply made a butt, as French masters too commonly were in that day, and spoke English very imperfectly. There was a Catholic family in the village, old maiden ladies we used to think; but I knew nothing but their name. I have of late years heard that there were one or two Catholic boys in the school; but either we were carefully kept from knowing this, or the knowledge of it made simply no impression on our minds. My brother will bear witness how free the school was from Catholic ideas.'[1]

In a sermon preached shortly after the restoration of the Roman Catholic hierarchy in England in 1850, Newman gives a more vivid account of how Catholics were regarded in England.

'Here a set of poor Irishmen, coming and going at harvest time, or a colony of them lodged in a miserable quarter of the vast

[1] J. H Newman. *Apologia Pro Vita Sua* (London, 1864), *op. cit.*, pp. 96–7.

metropolis. There perhaps an elderly person, seen walking in the streets, grave and solitary, and strange, though noble in bearing, and said to be of good family, and—a "Roman Catholic". An old-fashioned house of gloomy appearance, closed in with high walls, with an iron gate, and yews, and the report attaching to it that "Roman Catholics" lived there; but who they were, or what they did, or what was meant by calling them Roman Catholics no one could tell—though it had an unpleasant sound, and told of form and superstition.'[1]

Finally, in his *Lectures on the Present Position of Catholics in England*, Cardinal Newman explores the reasons which led to the building of this attitude of hostility and suspicion towards Catholics in England, an attitude which endured from the sixteenth to the first decades of the twentieth century and which in some places still endures. He begins by setting himself the task of explaining:

'. . . why it is, that, in this intelligent nation, and in this rational nineteenth century, we Catholics are so despised and hated by our own countrymen, with whom we have lived all our lives, that they are prompt to believe any story, however extravagant, that is told to our disadvantage; as if beyond a doubt we were, every one of us, either brutishly deluded or preternaturally hypocritical, and they themselves, on the contrary were in comparison of us absolute specimens of sagacity, wisdom, uprightness, manly virtue, and enlightened Christianity. . . . . I do but propose to investigate how Catholics come to be so trodden under foot, and spurned by a people which is endowed by nature with many great qualities, moral and intellectual; how it is that we are cried out against by the very stones, and bricks, and tiles, and chimney-pots of a populous busy place, such as this town which we inhabit.'[2]

Newman believed that the reasons which lay behind this attitude towards Catholicism on the part of the people of England were

[1] J. H. Newman. *The Second Spring* Sermon preached at the First Provincial Synod of Westminster, Oscott, 1852.
[2] J. H. Newman. *Lectures on the Present Position of Catholics in England* (London, 1908 edn.).

reasons of state, i.e. that political and national considerations prevented the Catholic Church from being heard in her own defence.

'She is considered too absurd to be inquired into, and too corrupt to be defended, and too dangerous to be treated with equity and fair dealing. She is the victim of a prejudice which perpetuates itself, and gives birth to what it feeds upon.'[1]

The centuries of anti-Roman propaganda; the identification of the Roman Catholic Church with corruption and evil on the religious level, and with treacherous designs to destroy the Protestant monarchy and replace it with a Catholic puppet manipulated by the Pope on the political level, had combined to instill in Englishmen an almost instinctively hostile reaction to all things papist. The Roman Catholic Church was equated, in English minds, with absolutism in both the spiritual and political fields. The Pope was regarded as a *political* enemy of England; he was thought of as an autocratic monarch, anxious to extend his sway over Britain. This is what had created the attitude of mind about which Newman complains.

The most celebrated anti-Catholic outburst occurred just in the middle of the nineteenth century at the time of the re-establishment of the Roman Catholic hierarchy in England and Wales. Given the prevailing climate of opinion on religious matters it would have been very surprising if some unfavourable reactions had not been experienced, but a number of circumstances combined to turn what would have been a strong protest into a violent exhibition of religious prejudice.[2] The attack was begun by *The Times* newspaper (14 October 1850), which concentrated on the appointment of Cardinal Wiseman as the new Archbishop of Westminster. The newspaper spoke of Wiseman as 'the new-fangled Archbishop of Westminster' and said that the Action of the Pope in conferring this title

'signifies no more than if the Pope had been pleased to confer on the editor of *The Tablet* the rank and title of the Duke of Smithfield [a London fish-market]. But if this appointment be not

[1] *Ibid.*
[2] See G. Albion. 'The Restoration of the Hierarchy' in *The English Catholics*, ed. G. Beck (London, 1950).

intended as a clumsy joke, we confess that we can only regard it as one of the grossest acts of folly and impertinence which the Court of Rome has ventured to commit since the Crown and people of England threw off its yoke'.[1]

In its issue of 19 October *The Times* went further and employed stronger language. It referred to an 'Italian priest' who was 'to parcel out the spiritual dominion of this country' and 'to restore a foreign usurpation over the consciences of men and to sow divisions in our political society by an undisguised and systematic hostility to the institutions most nearly identified with our national freedom and our national faith.'[2] In the same month the Papal Brief, restoring the hierarchy, and a pastoral letter written by Cardinal Wiseman in Rome before his departure for England, arrived in England and were published. The language in which they were written provoked a further outburst of violent indignation, this time not only from *The Times* newspaper but also from highly placed Anglican clergymen and leading statesmen, including Lord John Russell, the Prime Minister. The Pope was accused, by *The Times*, of aping 'the pretensions of a Hildebrand'; the Anglican Bishop of Durham protested at the 'insolent and insidious' action of the Pope, and Russell himself not only replied to the Bishop's protest in similar terms but made a speech in which he expressed the same sentiments.[3] Several other Bishops of the Established Church (throughout the month of November) made statements which, in the terms of abuse chosen, matched anything of the sixteenth century.

There were demonstrations also by the more humble in the land. Effigies of the Pope and of Wiseman were publicly burned, together with a document representing the Papal Brief. Catholic priests were abused and insulted—and sometimes attacked—in the streets, and there were demonstrations outside Catholic churches, sometimes culminating in the smashing of their windows. Many Catholics, remembering the Gordon riots, feared that this was just the preliminary stage of another period of prolonged and

[1] See G. Albion, *op. cit.*, pp. 97–8.
[2] *Ibid.*, p. 98.
[3] *Ibid.*, p. 99.

brutal violence, but the situation was changed by the action of Wiseman himself. He issued a pamphlet, *Appeal to the English People*, in which he explained frankly that the people had been deceived and misled; that his—Wiseman's—authority extended only over Catholics in the spiritual sphere and that it was a fallacy to suggest that he and the other bishops were claiming material possession of the districts marked out as their diocese, and that if the Catholic religion, which was essentially episcopal, was to be tolerated in England at all then, logically, permission had to be granted to establish a Catholic hierarchy.[1]

Wiseman deliberately addressed his appeal to popular sympathy, rather than to the educated and influential whom he regarded as having misled the people. As a result the circulation of his pamphlet was enormous: it appeared in full in five London dailies (with *The Times* devoting a large amount of space to it) and sold 30,000 copies. Its effect was immediate; the violence was quelled and the protest became much more subdued. It did not prevent Parliament from passing the Ecclesiastical Titles Bill on 7 February 1851 (by which, among other things, a penalty of £100 was inflicted on persons assuming titles to pretended sees in the United Kingdom), but it did help to forestall a repetition of the events of 1780. The Ecclesiastical Titles Bill, in fact, was never effectively operated and was quietly repealed twenty years later.

Enough evidence has been adduced in the preceding paragraphs to account for the isolation of the old Catholics from the remainder of English society. Attempts, first of all, to establish themselves as full citizens in their own land and, later, to establish their Church as a visible institution had been successful, but had been met with such violent displays of anti-Catholic feeling that these individuals must have been convinced that the days when they could hope to integrate fully with English society were far ahead. It was not only that the centuries of living under penal legislation had sapped the desire or the ability of these Catholics to take their place in English society but the fact that it was painfully evident that English society was still hostile to them that made them remain isolated.

The fact of their isolation from the urban Catholic groups is

[1] *Ibid.*, pp. 102–3.

simply explained. The only thing that the English Catholic country gentleman—or, for that matter, his tenants—had in common with the urban Catholic was his religion. The gentry felt that they had recognised the spiritual bond between them and the urban new-comers when they had subscribed to Catholic charities and, in some cases, had built churches in the new towns. In nationality, social class, upbringing and outlook the two sections of the Catholic Church were very different. It would have been too much to expect that either group would be conscious of the needs and aspirations of the other or that sufficiently close bonds could be established between them for them to work in harmony and understanding together. These points will, we think, become apparent when we deal with the urban Catholics in the remaining sections of this work.

# 3. Urban Catholics

The Catholics who lived in the great industrial towns of nineteenth-century England were, to a very large extent, immigrants from Ireland.

What sort of society were the immigrants coming into? They landed in a country convulsed by great social and economic changes—changes which involved the growth of huge new towns and the shifting of immense numbers of people from old centres to new. For centuries before the middle of the eighteenth century, the main industry in Britain had been the wool trade. Its centres were to be found in the West Country, Norfolk and—even before the so-called 'Industrial Revolution'—the West Riding of Yorkshire. The importance of the wool trade meant that the areas mentioned above became centres of relatively dense population so that by the beginning of the eighteenth century these districts, together with the great trading centre of London and certain ports like Bristol and Newcastle, had the heaviest concentrations of people living in them. In spite of this, by far the greater proportion of the inhabitants of Britain, in the middle of the eighteenth century, lived in the countryside.

During the nineteenth and twentieth centuries, these conditions have undergone a rapid and vital change. On the one hand there has been a tremendous growth in population and on the other a re-distribution of that population, which has involved the creation of great new urban centres. Thus, the first census of Great Britain, held in 1801, showed the population to be just below eleven millions; this had risen to sixteen and a half millions by 1831.[1] During those years the population of Lancashire grew by ninety-

[1] See census of Great Britain: volumes for the appropriate years.

eight per cent, the West Riding of Yorkshire by seventy-four per cent and there had been an even bigger increase in the population of Lanark in Scotland. The towns in the new industrial areas had shown an increase of even greater proportions than those already mentioned. For example, in 1770 Manchester contained 40,000 people, but by 1821 this figure had increaseg to 187,000; the towns of Leeds, Sheffield and Birmingham all doubled their population in thirty years.[1]

Beyond the confines of these great urban centres the whole face of the country changed. During the eighteenth century improved methods of agriculture had led to the enclosing of large areas of open fields so that by 1821 all that had been left of Britain's medieval fields and commons, about six million acres, had been enclosed. Parallel with these developments in agriculture had gone the growth of industry. Before the beginning of the Napoleonic wars in 1793, Britain's exports had ranged in value between £20 and £25 millions annually; by 1830 this figure had increased to around £70 millions. At the same time, iron production and the import of raw cotton for the textile industries had both multiplied several times over.[2]

This expansion in industry, and the consequent increase in the urban population, continued steadily throughout the nineteenth century and brought in its train a host of social problems. Large numbers of people were concentrated in the new towns and cities which had grown up on the coal-fields or near the centres of the manufacturing industries, and for many of these people—the labouring poor—the first half of the nineteenth century saw many periods of sharp suffering. It is true that an exaggerated picture can be drawn of the tribulations of the labouring classes in the great towns, and there is little doubt that the living conditions of the urban worker at this period may have compared well with those experienced by his parents and grandparents who worked on the land; nevertheless the working population of the new urban centres were well acquainted with the harsh and unpleasant side of life.

[1] *Ibid.*
[2] For works which deal with the general social and economic history of England and Wales in this period see Bibliography; in particular note the works of Ashton, T. S., Halevy, E., Clapham, J. H., Mantoux, P., and Redford, A.

The government, under the influence of the prevailing political and economic philosophy of 'laissez faire', not only made little attempt to protect the workers against exploitation by the employers but actually robbed them of the means of self defence through the early legislation against the Trade Unions.[1] The Act by which this was brought about—the Combination Act of 1799—forbade combinations among workmen or employers aimed at exercising 'restraint of trade'; there was also a fear in the government's mind that such organisations among the labouring class could be used for political means to bring about a 'convulsion' on the lines of the French Revolution. Even when the Combination Act was repealed in 1824, workmen attempting to form Trade Unions could be and were prosecuted under the Common Law on a charge of conspiracy. Nevertheless, some unions did exist in the first half of the nineteenth century, masquerading for the most part as benefit clubs and 'friendly societies', but their organisation was loose and their activities largely ineffectual. The Grand National Consolidated Trade Union formed by Robert Owen in the 1830's was short-lived and completely ineffective.

As a result of these circumstances, the labouring classes went through a period between 1815 and 1850 when wage rates were being driven down through the influx of cheap labour from Ireland, when factory hours were inordinately long—in many cases amounting to fourteen or sixteen hours a day—when women and children worked in bad conditions in factories and mines and when living conditions in many new towns were sordid in the extreme. Many efforts were made by charitable individuals to relieve the effects of these conditions upon the poor, but the work of such people made little impression on the problem as a whole.

---

[1] It should be stated, in order to achieve some balance in judgement, that the government and the employers for the most part acted in the firm conviction that what they were doing was economically necessary. They thought that to allow the capitalist manufacturer and employer to pursue his own ends without hindrance was the only way to ensure prosperity for all. Only by being permitted to increase his own wealth was the individual likely to expand his enterprises and hence provide increased work and more employment for others. Anything which interfered with this freedom—such as attempts by workmen to restrict hours of work and to increase wages—was likely to interfere with the free development of individual enterprises and hence was wrong.

The only weapon which the poor possessed to make any effective protest against these circumstances was violence. During the first forty years of the nineteenth century there were outbreaks of rioting among farmworkers and machine-breaking among factory employees. However, it is perhaps the Chartist movement which reflects most accurately the mood and temper of the working class in the 1830's and 1840's—a mixed feeling of revolt and confusion as to the most effective way to make their protest achieve some practical result. Chartism assembled all the protests that had been made against the wretched conditions of the working class and brought them forcibly to the notice of the nation. This was the main achievement of the movement for its effectiveness in practical spheres was ruined by factions amongst the leaders and disagreement over the means—political or industrial, constitutional or violent—by which its ends were to be achieved. Eventually the supporters of violent means overcame the moderates and in 1839 there were riots in the Midlands and an abortive uprising in South Wales. After 1839, with a brief revival in 1848, Chartism gradually petered out and lost any effectiveness that it may have possessed.

In the second half of the nineteenth century the working class began to organise an effective means of self-protection. A much more efficient form of trade union made its appearance in 1851 with the foundation of the Amalgamated Society of Engineers—a well-organised body run by full-time paid officials and catering for the workers in one craft only (as opposed to Owen's Grand National Consolidated Trade Union which had tried to combine all workers, whatever their trade, into one organisation). This union provided the model for others which were formed during the second half of the century. The years following the Royal Commission on Trade Unions in 1867 saw legislation, particularly during the period 1870–5, which put the unions on a firm basis, protected their funds and gave them the power to use the strike weapon effectively. Their position was further strengthened by the legislation in the first two decades of the twentieth century which recognised that a union could not be sued by an employer for loss of trade incurred as a result of a strike, and which gave unions the right to extract a political levy from its members unless they specifically 'contracted out' of paying it.

This establishment of Trade Unions was only one aspect of the social revolution which was taking place in the nineteenth century. Throughout the period legislation was introduced, haphazardly it must be admitted, by successive governments in order to improve the condition of the working classes. Such legislation was produced mainly as the result of popular agitation combined with the philanthropic leanings of prominent individuals; it was not the result of any deliberate party policy put into operation by the government of the day.

The peak period for government activity in this sphere was the twenty-five years after 1850. As well as the Trade Union legislation enacted between 1867 and 1875 the 'friendly' and 'co-operative' societies received a new legal protection and could operate more effectively among the working class from whom they drew their membership. Some attempt had been made to enforce government control over factories and workshops before 1850 but these efforts had been rendered ineffective largely because of the lack of an adequate, independent inspectorate to ensure that the regulations were obeyed—often a number of the magistrates who composed the inspectorate were employers. After 1850 an efficient inspectorate was created and thus the Ten Hours Act, introduced in 1847 and amended in 1853, began to be enforced properly and helped a great deal in improving the life of the working man by ensuring that no individual worked for more than ten hours a day.

Government control was gradually extended over industries other than coal-mining and the textile trades, to which the first acts had been originally confined, but some of the most flagrant abuses in every branch of the manufacturing industries were not stamped out until the earlier years of the twentieth century. During this period, also, the new municipal corporations which controlled the urban areas began to make use of the powers they held to improve the living standards of their citizens. Medical officers of health were appointed to make sure that the sanitary conditions were satisfactory; these officials working together did a tremendous amount to improve the living conditions of the poorer classes and to wipe out the menace of typhus and cholera which scourged the great towns of Britain in the middle of the nineteenth century. Apart from this remedying of basic evils the corporations set about providing the amenities of civilised living by building art galleries and museums, laying out public parks and establishing free lending libraries and reading rooms.

Two more aspects of this third quarter of the nineteenth century need to be mentioned before this section of the work is closed. There gradually developed during this time a new interest in political circles—a concern for popular education. In 1870 Parliament passed legislation which set up elementary schools which were to be built, equipped and maintained out of public funds and which would provide, at a very small cost, basic grounding in reading, writing and arithmetic for the children of the poor. This was a tremendous advance for it meant that the labourer of 1875 was much better situated than his father had been and that he could have some small confidence in the prospects for his children. Finally, in 1872 the urban workman achieved the dignity of full citizenship. In 1867 he had been given a vote in parliamentary and municipal elections and in the appointment of the Guardians of the Poor; in 1872 the Ballot Act gave him the right to make his vote in secret so that no pressure could be brought upon him to vote in any way other than he personally chose. In all these developments the Catholic community played little or no part.

GROWTH OF URBAN POPULATION

The large concentrations of population in the urban areas of Great Britain created a new form of industrial society in which new patterns of living evolved. In order to see how they developed it is necessary to study more closely the make-up of these urban communities and in particular to study the growth in the towns of the groups of Irish immigrants who were to form the largest part of the Catholic community in the country.

The growth of population in Great Britain during the nineteenth and twentieth centuries was due, largely, to a natural increase and not to immigration from other countries. The relative growth of population in the great towns resulted from the movement of people from rural areas who came to the town in search of work and increased wages.[1] The cotton industry, for example, developed rapidly and led to the growth of Manchester around which it was centred. In this particular industry the transition to power-weaving displaced many hand-loom weavers and the absorption of the latter into factory industry was too slow to prevent widespread distress amongst them, a distress that was aggravated by the continually increased immigration of Irish weavers. The woollen and worsted industries were becoming concentrated in the West Riding of Yorkshire as a result of the decline of the ancient clothing districts of East Anglia and the West Country. Migration from East Anglia and the West Country which followed this decline was directed mainly towards London and South Wales.

Studies of the iron and coal industries throw light on this question of the movement of labour from the rural districts into the industrial areas.[2] In the South Wales area, for example, there is a distinction to be drawn between the movement of skilled and unskilled labour. There was a short-distance movement of skilled labour due mainly to the concentration of the greater part of the copper smelting and tinplate industries on the coal-field itself, and to the gradual development of those industries and the relatively small number of skilled workmen employed. In the iron and coal industries a similar short-distance movement was common, with iron workers and colliers moving from one South Wales valley to the next, as works were established and individual concerns either expanded or contracted.[3]

Unskilled labour tended to move much longer distances. These workers were drawn mainly from the agricultural counties surrounding the new towns or the coal-fields, and the number of recruits from each county decreases as the distance of the county from the industrial centre increases. In South Wales, if we may once more take this area as an example, large numbers of unskilled labourers moved into the Glamorgan coal-field from Pembrokeshire

[1] See Redford, A. *Labour Migration in England, 1800–1850* (Manchester, 1926).
[2] See, for example, A. H. John, *The Industria lDevelopment of South Wales* (University of Wales Press, 1950).
[3] *Ibid.*

(which had experienced no movement of skilled men), Carmarthen-
shire, Brecknockshire and Cardiganshire and lesser numbers came
from English counties. This movement was not simply a drift;
there was a long and continuous depopulation of the hill country
of West Wales.[1]

IRISH IMMIGRATION TO URBAN AREAS

Once in the towns, these migrants from the country districts
were joined by immigrants from Ireland. Throughout the nineteenth century the rate of immigration from Ireland into Britain
was maintained at a high level, with a considerable increase after
the famine years of 1845–8. At all times since 1841 the principal
causes of this immigration have been economic.[2] The bulk of
Ireland's population, which had increased to eight millions by
1845 was dependent on the land for a living and the potato for
food.[3] Distress and unemployment on the land could find no outlet
for there was no industry to absorb the surplus workers, and this
factor provided the main impetus for emigration. Contemporary
official reports give a vivid picture of the conditions which helped
to stimulate the flight from Ireland. In 1830, for instance, it was
noted that as a result of the division and sub-division of land-
holdings—so that the sons of the family could have a plot of land
to provide a livelihood for their own families—the land was cut up
and abused by bad tillage.[4] This was followed by a deterioration in
the soil which led, in turn, to the potato crop becoming uncertain.
To add to the people's miseries their living conditions were very
poor; the Report describes the cabins in which they lived as
'. . . the most miserable and wretched to be seen, enough to give
them fever and sickness which it does in many cases.'[5]

More dramatic is the actual evidence given by witnesses before
the various Commissions which were held about this time to

[1] *Ibid.*
[2] G. O'Brien: *The Economic History of Ireland from the Union to the Famine*
(London, 1921).
[3] See *Commission on Emigration and Other Population Problems: 1948–1954,
Reports, op. cit.*
[4] *Report of the Select Committee on the State of the Poor in Ireland, 1830*, p. 7.
[5] *Ibid.*

enquire into the state of affairs in Ireland. In 1835, for instance, Father P. Walsh, of Connaught in County Galway, said:

'There are, in my part of the Union (which is about a third of it) 400 persons not able to get constant employment; none of them get regular work; each of them would be employed three months at their own work, sowing their con-acre and tilling their little plots; during the remaining nine there is scarcely anything for them to earn; there are very few employers in that district. They are not able to eat an egg; they must sell it, and try to pay for the con-acre by their price, that of their little pig, and sometimes a little flax; by this means they support themselves in half starvation. I have known a hundred instances of persons not having more than one meal a day during the month of July last; for the two previous months they used great economy, trying to make their provisions last; they used two very moderate meals a day.'[1]

To this may be added the remarks of another witness, J. O'Flaherty who gave evidence before the Commissioners at the same time. He said:

'There are nine or ten families in my village whom I know to be without half enough to eat during the summer; I do not mean one summer in particular, but every summer.'[2]

These were not isolated examples; similar evidence was given by witnesses from Counties Mayo, Roscommon and Sligo and from Leinster, Munster and Ulster.[3] They have been quoted here not only to demonstrate the reasons why the Irish emigrated in such numbers during the period in question but because such conditions endured over a long period of time, must have had an effect on the immigrants' attitude to the sort of employment, wages and living conditions that they would be prepared to accept in this country. This point will be considered in more detail later in the book.

While economic conditions in Ireland stimulated emigration, the state of the British economy encouraged immigration. Unskilled labour was required for the construction of docks, railways and

---

[1] *First Report from His Majesty's Commissioners for inquiring into the condition of the Poorer Classes in Ireland*, 1835.
[2] *Ibid.*                                    [3] *Ibid.*

industrial plants and the Irish immigrants were plentiful and suitable. According to one observer the Irish workman was superior to the English or Scottish because of his 'willingness, alacrity and perseverance in the severest, the most irksome and most disagreeable kinds of coarse labour . . .' moreover, 'though in Ireland a labourer does not perform half so much work in a day for eightpence as an English labourer does for sixpence, yet when he is stimulated by high wages he is found to exert an energy and zeal which cannot easily be surpassed.'[1]

Having landed in Britain the immigrants, or, at least, the greater proportion of them, made at once for the towns. A small number settled on the land but most of them established themselves in the new urban areas—the three chief centres of settlement being Lancashire, Glasgow and London. Throughout the first half of the nineteenth century, Lancashire contained a greater number of Irish settlers than any other county, the majority of these immigrants being concentrated in the region of Liverpool and Manchester. In Scotland the Irish were to be found mainly in Glasgow, Greenock, Dundee, Edinburgh and Paisley. Many of those who left Ireland to escape the effects of the great famine settled in the ports of Britain where they first landed.[2]

The nature of the work which the inhabitants of the new towns entered varied, naturally, with the prevailing type of industry in the immediate area. One invariable feature, however, which does emerge from the contemporary evidence is that the Irish immigrants were prepared to undertake jobs which the native workers found unattractive. It is common to find the immigrants engaged as unskilled artisans. A few examples taken from various parts of the country should be sufficient to make this point clear. Many of the immigrants were employed on public works, i.e. the building of docks, railways and canals and the construction of roads, while others found employment in menial tasks connected with other trades. In London, for instance, many Irish were found among the lowest class of builders' labourers while in Lancashire and the West Riding of Yorkshire they worked as hodmen. In Paisley, in

[1] G. C. Lewis in his *Report for the Poor Law Commission, 1830.*
[2] See *Commission on Emigration, op. cit.*

Scotland, the Irish were brought in as cotton spinners, and in the cotton and textile trades generally the Irish were to be found among the hand-loom weavers. In the coal and iron industries a great deal of coarse labour was done by the Irish, especially in Scotland, and in Liverpool many of the Irish living there were employed in soap boiling. Apart from these jobs in industry a number of the immigrants supported themselves by keeping lodging-houses or beerhouses or travelled the countryside making a living as pedlars. The wages that the immigrants earned compared very favourably with those they had been accustomed to in Ireland, e.g. in Ireland the agricultural labourer earned between sixpence and one shilling a day while in England he could get up to twelve shillings a week; as a builders' labourer his wage would increase to between sixteen shillings and eighteen shillings a week.[1]

What was the standard of living achieved by the immigrants in the first sixty years of the nineteenth century? It is difficult to give a precise answer to this question, but it is apparent from the evidence available that although the native British workmen did not have a high standard of living, the Irish were prepared to accept an even lower standard and composed a class which was in the nature of a sub-strata of society, e.g. in Manchester and Preston the majority of the cellar-dwellers were Irish.[2] In fact it is apparent from contemporary official reports that both type of work and place of residence tended very strongly to separate the immigrants from the native working class; this in turn meant that the Catholic groups began their existence in the towns in a condition of social isolation. This 'social' aspect of the early life of the re-established Catholic Church in Britain will be gone into much more thoroughly in the next section, but the fact of this division of Catholics from their neighbours can be stated now.

### PATTERN OF LIVING IN WORKING-CLASS AREAS

We cannot really make the statement that the settlements of Catholics in the urban areas developed in isolation from the main

[1] See Redford, A., *op. cit.*
[2] See *Report of the Select Committee on Poor Removal*, 1854.

working-class groups without making some mention of the pattern of living which was emerging among those groups. It is not possible to give a picture of the country as a whole but some impressions can be gained from contemporary sources, again restricting the choice of evidence to that taken from official reports of one sort or another. Such reports do not make really entertaining reading but are more likely to be reliable sources of evidence than the romanticised versions given by novelists of the period.

The houses that the workers occupied did not vary a great deal in size, amenities and rent between one town and another. In Birmingham, for instance, there was, in the middle of the nineteenth century, a large number of cottage properties grouped together in suburbs close to the centres of industry.[1] A typical cottage possessed two rooms on the ground floor—parlour and kitchen—and two bedrooms on the first floor. The amenities included a washhouse, a privy and a cesspool. The rent for such a house would be approximately five shillings a week. It was likely that both the husband and the wife were employed in industry and that the children were sent out to earn once they had passed their sixth or seventh birthday. Wages varied according to the industry in which the worker was employed and to his personal status as skilled or unskilled. Many employed as labourers in the building trades, for instance, would receive a wage in the region of fifteen shillings a week; others, in the manufacturing industries, received up to forty shillings a week. The wives earned between ten and fourteen shillings a week.[2]

Work was arduous and hours were long, and the facilities for recreation for working families in the new towns were few. For many husbands and wives their only escape from the dreary monotony of their everyday existence was to be found in the public houses, where alcohol was plentiful and cheap. Hence drunkenness was a much more prominent feature of town life than it is today and provided the town authorities with abundant opportunities for commenting on the improvidence and intemperance

---

[1] See Evidence of the district medical officer of Birmingham in *Report to the General Board of Health on the Town of Birmingham*, 1849.
[2] *Ibid.*

of the working classes.[1] Many public houses had clubs attached
to them which met on their premises. Such clubs catered for
both men and women and made valiant attempts to provide the
social life so sadly lacking; they generally met once a month and
had an annual dinner, the latter sometimes being preceded by
celebrations during the day which often included a procession to
church or chapel. The cost for such a day's enjoyment was about
five shillings for each member, including the dinner.[2]

At public holidays, particularly Whitsun, it was the custom in
Birmingham, as in many other areas, especially in the north of
England, for whole neighbourhoods to promenade in their finery.
These Whit walks were an excellent opportunity for the whole
family to display themselves in their 'Sunday best' and to demonstrate their solidarity with their neighbours and workmates. The
District Medical Officer of Birmingham, describing such a display,
says '. . . they marshal themselves into a procession, with bands of
music, colours, flags and banners dispersed along their ranks and each
man or woman is ornamented with sashes or rosettes of ribbons'.[3]

Not all communal activity among the working class was aimed at
recreation. Apart from supporting political movements aimed at
reform and engaging in the activities of the early trade unions—
two aspects of working-class life already briefly mentioned and to be
dealt with again in a later section—men and women in the new
towns helped in the formation of a multitude of 'friendly societies'.
These organisations had two basic purposes—to bring their
members together to strengthen the social bond between them,
and to provide, through small cash subscriptions, insurance against
sickness, unemployment and death. In Birmingham alone there
were 213 of these friendly societies, 159 of which held their
meetings in inns, public houses or beer shops. The remainder met
in the more sedate atmosphere of school-rooms or rooms attached
to churches or chapels. The titles given to these societies are sometimes a straightforward indication of their aims, as in the 'Brotherly
Benefits Society', the 'Sick Man's Friend Society' or the
'Abstainers' Gift Society'; other names are more romantic and
intriguing—the 'Honourable Knights of the Wood' and the

[1] *Ibid.*                    [2] *Ibid.*                    [3] *Ibid.*

'Modern Druids'.[1] One is not quite sure in which category to put the 'Rational Sick and Burial Society'.

The picture which emerges from all this is of the development of a community spirit among people who had left areas where they had roots and traditions and who had to create something to take their place. Their task was made easier by the circumstances which shaped their new environment; they were thrown together in the settlements around factories, mines and mills, and work and home were linked closely together. A close alliance like this between place of work and home meant that friendships begun at work could be carried on during leisure hours and made it more likely that a common bond between people living in the same area could be established. The links were made stronger by the social clubs already mentioned and by the fact that in order to protect themselves against the dangers of financial insecurity the workers were obliged to co-operate in the friendly societies.

On another plane the pressure to co-operate with one another was felt. They had great things to fight for—political rights and better living and working conditions. These could only be achieved by united effort and through such organisations as trade unions and the associations like those which formed the Chartist movement. The emphasis all the time had to be on unity, brotherhood and solidarity and there was a constant pressure on the workers to identify themselves with their 'class'. For the individual born into such circumstances all this meant security. He went to school with children from the same street, played with them in that street and, when the time came, the likelihood was that his wife would be from the same area and would expect the new home to be within easy reach of her parents. For the worker and his family the world was populated by comrades and neighbours, people who knew you and respected you. Such a world faced constantly the threat of material insecurity—poverty caused by unemployment, sickness or death—but these were problems common to all and faced by all. What the working-class community provided for its members was roots, a basis for life, a means of self-identification, a sense of 'belonging' somewhere.

[1] *Ibid.*

# 4. Catholics and their Neighbours: General Considerations

At this stage it is necessary to refer back to the statement made at the beginning of Chapter 2—that the Catholic community in this country is largely an immigrant community and that it is important to understand something of its relationships with the rest of urban society in Britain if one is fully to appreciate the dilemma of the present-day Catholic. An examination of some urban Catholic groups will help to indicate why they largely held aloof from their neighbours; an aloofness that was evident in many forms but that was particularly noticeable in the field of political and social reform. The developments indicated in an earlier section, such as the movements for reform among the working classes—in particular Chartism and Trade Unionism—took place without the active help of the Catholic body as a whole. In fact the immigrant Irish actively opposed Chartist activity in Manchester and South Wales,[1] allowed themselves to be used as strike-breakers—e.g. at Preston in 1854[2]—and engaged in bitter and bloody battles with the native workmen in many areas of Britain.[3] These activities have led to the immigrants being accused of breaking up the solidarity of the labouring classes and hindering the growth of a stable labour organisation in Britain. There is undoubtedly some justification for such an accusation, but there is little point in levelling it without at the same time attempting to discover the root causes of the immigrants' behaviour. At a superficial examination it seems to be

[1] For a well-documented account of this opposition on the part of the Manchester Irish to Chartism see McCord, N., *The Anti-Corn Law League* (London, 1958), pp. 99–103. For disturbances in South Wales, see Evans, E. W., *The miners of South Wales* (University of Wales, 1961).

[2] See Redford, A., *op. cit.*

[3] See Halévy, E., *A History of the English People in the 19th Century*, vol. III (in particular pp. 7ff and pp. 152–3).

entirely out of character. How could it possibly happen that in the large towns of Britain in the nineteenth century there were large groups of Catholics whose immediate forefathers had suffered at the hands of the English government, who had been driven by hunger from their homeland and forced to seek a living in an alien land, and who yet were not prepared to support or encourage popular movements to reform the government and who refused to throw in their lot with their neighbours and workmates? There is some examination of the reason for the non-participation of Catholics in political activity in Section 6 of this study; what we are concerned with in this section is to attempt to bring out the root causes of the isolation of the urban Catholic communities.

The development of most urban Catholic groups falls into two main phases—a period when the group is effectively isolated and contact with the rest of urban society is small, and a period when this isolation is being broken down. It is with this former period that we shall be most concerned in this section for the process of 'integration' of Catholics is only just beginning and some of its implications are described in the last section of this book.

The causes of isolation of the Catholic communities are to be found in influences which operated both inside and outside the communities themselves. The opposition to Catholics from outside was based largely on three grounds—religious, social and national. These three were linked, often inextricably, to produce a feeling of hostility towards the newcomers, but they have been divided in order to demonstrate more clearly the way in which different forces can operate to the same end, in this case the isolation of a group of people from their neighbours. Of these three factors, religion was the first and most important. It has already been made plain, that at the start of the nineteenth century many people in different parts of the country looked with great apprehension on the prospect of a restoration of Catholicism and were prepared to exert as much pressure as possible to prevent it. The incidents connected with the Gordon riots, and the violent reaction to the news of the restoration of the Roman Catholic hierarchy in Britain in the middle of the nineteenth century have already been dealt with. The point that can be made, however, is that this feeling was not confined to a drunken mob led by a semi-lunatic peer nor to interested political circles in London. Newspapers in the 1820's frequently carried reports of meetings held to protest at the possible granting of some relief to Catholics. One paper, for instance, carried reports of four such meetings, held at Spitalfields, Ash, Teignmouth and Dawlish. Of the meeting at Ash it says:

'Agreeable to previous notice, a numerous and respectable Meeting of the inhabitants of Ash, next Sandwich, assembled on Friday last to consider the propriety of petitioning the Senate on the Catholic Question. A Petition to both Houses of Parliament was unanimously agreed to. The petition to the House of Lords is to be entrusted to the marquis of Camden, and the one to the Commons to Sir Edw. Knatchbull.'[1]

The tone of the other reports is similar to this; there is no attempt on the part of the paper itself to use the report as a means of purveying anti-Catholic propaganda.

Not all the editors of provincial newspapers exercised the same restraint. In one such newspaper, for instance, there appeared, in April 1842, the following editorial comment following a prolonged controversy between an Anglican clergyman and a Catholic priest:

'We now leave the subject, again expressing our heartfelt pleasure that whilst Roman Catholicism is endeavouring to raise its hydra head, the Church of England possesses men who will go forth fearlessly to encounter the monster, and prevent the moral and spiritual desolation which would be caused by its pestilential breath.'[2]

In 1861 the same journal felt that the time was ripe to call the attention of its readers once more to the danger which existed in their midst. The publication of the *Catholic Directory* for that year showed an increase in the number of Catholic clergy and laity in England and Wales and the newspaper seized on this. An article under the heading 'Alarming increase of popery in Great Britain' gave details of the strength of the Church and instructs readers that they should

[1] *The Cambrian*, 16 April, 1825.
[2] *Cardiff and Merthyr Guardian*, April, 1842.

'. . . with one heart and mind unite in opposition to Popish error and in defence of Protestant truth, and never cease their exertions until the glad sound is heard—Babylon the great is fallen to rise no more for ever.'[1]

The prevailing note behind this type of newspaper comment is fear. The image of Catholicism had been distorted by centuries of regarding the Pope as a personal enemy of Britain, waiting with his legions to overcome Protestantism and to place the country under his domination. It was all too easy to regard Catholicism as a menace, religious and political, and, consequently, to regard those members of the Catholic Church, who were entering Britain in a steady stream from Ireland, as alien and possibly dangerous. It is not surprising, then, that urban Catholics were soon to discover that their religion was to play a prominent part in isolating them from the remainder of the new community they had entered. It is not without significance in this connection, that the churches which the immigrants built in their 'settlements' often became the focal point of the riots that took place between the Irish and their new working-class neighbours. The Church stood as the symbol of all that was 'different' about the newcomers, and in one such riot at least a determined effort was made to burn down the building itself.[2]

Social antagonism came from many different quarters. The attitude of the local authorities comes through very strongly in the official reports of the time dealing with the affairs of the working classes. As the following examples will show, the immigrants were constantly castigated for their way of life and accused of introducing all sorts of evils into the towns. The District Medical Officer of Birmingham, writing in 1849, says:

'There has been no disease in my district since the 1st. of November of either an epidemic or endemic character, which perhaps is rather to be surprised at considering the locality and the class of people living in it, consisting as it does chiefly of

[1] *Ibid.*, April, 1861.
[2] See below.

the low Irish whose habits generally are of the most filthy kind. . . .'[1]

The Sanitary Inspector of the same town added that he felt that the increase in 'low fever' was partly the consequence of 'an influx of Irish who have brought the disease with them.'[2]

This tendency to single out the Irish for special comment is taken a stage further in other official Reports; evidence like the following relegates the immigrants to a special class and highlights the difference between them and the English working class:

'. . . you have a large body of Irish people in the town of Manchester, a great many thousands, and in certain parishes in London; their habits are not the same as those of the English labourers; they do not feed so well, and they are to be found in a destitute neighbourhood and congregating in the lowest locality. Theirs is the lowest labour; the hodman is an Irishman, while his master is an Englishman, and seven out of ten of those doing the commonest labour down this river are Irish. Those men frequent the worst localities, and the cheapest lodgings. If you look at the returns (for poor removal) for a very small number of parishes, you will see that they are contributing 9/10ths. of the removals of Irish poor. Some 20 or 30 parishes contain them All . . .'[3]

The tendency of the immigrants to live together, to occupy what was generally recognised as the poorest class of property and to engage in the most menial of tasks was not confined to one part of the country or even to the major cities.

Evidence exists of the establishment of an Irish colony at Batley in Yorkshire, and of a group of Irish at Birstal. In the latter town they were housed in a group of cottages which the owners had been about to pull down and rebuild. A contractor who was building a branch railway line bought the cottages, put them in a state of

---

[1] *Report to the General Board of Health on a Preliminary Inquiry into the Sewerage, Drainage, and Supply of Water, and the Sanitary Conditions of the Inhabitants of the Borough of Birmingham, May 1849*, evidence of Mr. Sproston, district medical officer, p. 22.

[2] *Ibid.*, evidence of J. Hodgson, medical sanitary inspector, p. 88.

[3] *Report of the Select Committee on Poor Removal, 1854*, evidence of R. Pashley.

temporary repair and housed a number of Irish labourers in them. When the work on the railway was completed, the Irish refused to move on but insisted on remaining in Birstal because 'they liked the quarters too well' and would 'try to earn their livelihood by any description of labour which they were capable of doing . . .'[1] Witnesses said that they discovered

'in some cottages as many as thirty people residing in the same cottage, the cottage consisting only of a low room and a chamber above; and we found them altogether in a very different state from what English labourers are in that part of the country.'[2]

Witnesses at these enquiries produced similar evidence of the formation of separate Irish communities all over the country from Berwick to London. In Berwick a small group of the immigrants had occupied a particular part of the town; their living habits were 'squalid' and they had displaced the English tenants.[3] In Bradford, where it was claimed, in 1855, that there were about twenty thousand Irish, the immigrants were chiefly employed as wool-combers. The witness from this town, claimed that as well as having 'low habits' the Irish were 'turbulent and disorderly'; he obviously had strong feelings on the matter for he had gone to the trouble to prepare statistics to illustrate his point. These revealed that of nine hundred prisoners taken into custody in 1854, five hundred were English—1/200 of the English population—and four hundred were Irish—1/50th of the Irish population. The witness was further of the opinion that if it were not for the Irish, the police force, which stood at one hundred and ten, might be reduced to a dozen men.[4]

Some of the evidence in these reports is actively hostile to the Irish; some, while noting their poor living standards, is sympathetic. But all the officials who made statements to the Commissions have this in common—that they relegate the Irish to a social standing below that of the native working class and consider them as a group apart. They were a new and alien factor in the

---

[1] *Report of the Select Committee on Poor Removal, 1855*, evidence of J. Ellison.
[2] *Ibid.*
[3] *Ibid.*, evidence of E. Willoby.
[4] *Ibid.*, evidence of J. Darlington.

social structure of England. The attitude implied in this is expressed very vividly in some of the newspaper comment at the time. The *Cardiff and Merthyr Guardian* for instance, in the 1840's, often took pains to point out to its readers that most of the social evils in the town resulted from the influx of immigrants and could not be eradicated until the habits of the latter had been changed and their immigration checked. In April 1849 in an article dealing with the problems of a particular area of Cardiff, the *Guardian* commented that

> 'Those cottages tend to invite a pauper race to make the town their headquarters, while they do not, generally speaking, contribute towards those funds from which the poor draw their means of subsistence.'[1]

In its issue of the following week, in a passage under the heading 'The Irish Plague' the newspaper mentions the fact that 'upwards of fifty miserable Irish wretches, in a most deplorable plight, were landed on Penarth beach and proceeded on to Cardiff. Some check,' the article continues, 'must be put to the thousands of Irish paupers who flock into the country.' The question of the control of immigration into Britain is one of burning interest today and we have been confronted with sufficient evidence to show that it is a matter which can arouse deep passions. At no time in the current debate, however, has a newspaper dared to use the intemperate language displayed in the examples just quoted and it would be unthinkable that a public official should report in a vein of thinly concealed contempt on the living conditions of present-day immigrants. It is easy to see why, in this context, the nineteenth-century Irish immigrants should feel that the authorities and the middle classes generally, whose opinions were reflected in the newspapers, were unsympathetic to their problems and hostile to their presence.

It was not long before it became evident that this hostility was not restricted to the substantial classes in society. The most violently expressed opposition to the newcomers came from their immediate neighbours—the working people with whom they had to share the same areas in the towns. The basis of this opposition

[1] *Op. cit.*, April, 1849.

appears to have been primarily economic; English workmen regarded the influx of Irishmen as a threat to their livelihood and to the living standards which they were struggling to achieve. The immigrants did not 'fit in' with their neighbours—they did not share the same background or the same aspirations. They had come from conditions of degradation and semi-starvation and were prepared to accept little in return for the opportunity to work and to support their families. The result was that they were ready to accept wages and conditions of work which were quite unacceptable to the native workmen. The employers, in many cases, were quick to recognise this and used Irish labour to lower rates of pay and to break strikes.

It was this refusal of the Irish workmen to identify himself with his English counterpart, and his readiness to accept a lower offer from the employer that provoked the outbreaks of violence described below. I have chosen the samples that follow because they bring out vividly, in the language of contemporary observers, the points that have been made; the examples are restricted to one area—South Wales—but they were repeated in similar form in many parts of the country—London, Lancashire and Yorkshire among them.[1]

On 10 May 1834, the newspaper *The Merlin* carried the following headline:

'Serious Disturbances at the Iron Works' Pontypool, May 9th. followed by this account:

'A deadly feud has for some time existed at the Varteg Iron Works, between the Welsh and Irish operatives, in consequence of the latter accepting less than the standard prices for their labour; and on Sunday evening last, a determination was entered into by the former to eject the obnoxious men *vi et armis*. An alarming affray was the natural consequence, and the Irishmen were at length compelled by superior numbers to retreat from the works . . . Another party sought shelter in the house of a man named John Morgan of Garndeffarth, but the infuriated Welshmen, during the night, made a combined attack upon the

[1] See Halévy, *op. cit.*, also *Report of the Select Committee on Poor Removal, 1855, op. cit.*

premises, and desisted not until they had rased the house to the ground.'[1]

The ironmasters themselves had to intervene in order to restore calm, but this was not achieved until they had sworn in one hundred special constables.

This riot was sparked off by the immigrants accepting lower rates of pay than the native workers were demanding. The following account describes disturbances in South Wales following the use of Irish labour to break a strike at a colliery:

'In November 1857 notice of a reduction of threepence per ton was given by the master owing to the slackness of trade. This reduction was only to last for three months if accepted peaceably. Being ill-advised however, the men brought their tools out. About the beginning of January the masters intimated that if the men returned to work in three days they would be allowed to do so at the announced reduction of threepence per ton, but if not that they would insist upon a reduction of fourpence per ton. The workmen would not agree to this offer, but in a fortnight afterwards were glad to return to work at a reduction of fourpence per ton.

During this last strike a number of Irishmen had been brought to work at the Bute Merthyr Colliery. This created a bitter feeling in the Welsh colliers towards them snd when the latter resumed work frequent quarrels took place between the two parties. However no serious rupture took place until one Saturday night in August (1857) when, after a drinking bout, the Irishmen became aggressive and insulting and this brought about a general fight, which in the end forced the Irishmen to beat a hasty retreat to their barracks. On the following Sunday night the fight was renewed and more bitterly as stones were freely thrown by both parties and some shots were fired. The Welsh determined to bring matters to an issue, and, at daylight on Monday, despatched messengers to the other villages in the valley for assistance. Before breakfast some 150 colliers marched

---

[1] *The Merlin*, 10 May, 1834. This incident is only one of a number described by this newspaper during these years.

up to Treherbert in an orderly procession, but all armed with some handy weapon. They crossed the river and, entering the Irishmen's barracks, smashed all the crockery-ware and drove the Irishmen out before them. The latter, seeing that resistance would be useless, reluctantly did as they were bid. One or two who felt an inclination to resent the intrusion were rather severely handled. The Irishmen were then ordered to march down the valley. The arrival of some policemen on the scene gave them a short respite; but the experience of the morning convinced them that it would not be advisable for them to remain there any longer and they left the neighbourhood— some making their way over the mountain to Aberdare whilst others followed the road to Pontypridd. It is said that very few Irishmen were to be found in any part of the valley for many years after this event.'[1]

Such events have long-lasting effects. They become part of the folk lore of an area; they are remembered and passed on from one generation to another, with suitable embellishments, as cautionary tales. The divisions they cause are hardened and perpetuated until they become accepted as natural. Public attacks upon their religion in the press, physical attacks upon their persons and property by their neighbours and workmates and their relegation by the authorities to the lowest position on the social scale, produced the inevitable reaction amongst the immigrants. The development of the Catholic immigrant communities in Britain follows a common pattern—withdrawal as far as possible from contact with their neighbours and the building of an independent community life.

[1] Account found in manuscript number M.S.4378, pp. 86–7, University of Wales Library, Aberystwyth.

# 5. Development of an Urban Community: Catholics in Cardiff

It is convenient at this stage to examine closely one example of a Catholic urban community in order to bring out in detail all the aspects that have so far been touched upon for the country as a whole. In the following account of the development of the Catholic community in the town of Cardiff may be seen vividly the operation of all the factors which went towards the building of an isolated and homogenous urban Catholic group; and the evidence already quoted indicates the existence of these factors in urban areas throughout England.

The picture which emerges from the following description of the Catholic group in Cardiff is one which is of considerable assistance in helping to analyse the process by which the Catholic urban populations are becoming assimilated with the larger groups within which they are situated. The study of Cardiff shows the initial separation of the immigrant group from its neighbours, the development of the settlement while still in a state of isolation, and, finally, the symptoms of the breakdown of this isolation.

The evidence put forward of the development of the Catholic settlement also helps to illustrate the nature of this isolation, and this in its turn helps to bring out the basic reasons for the development of a Catholic settlement which in many respects was apart from its non-Catholic neighbours and fellow-townspeople. In the first place the delineation of the Cardiff community shows that isolation meant far more than physical separation—although this factor was at first certainly present. The separation from their fellows was a matter, at first, as much of social status as of the fact of their occupying a different and easily identifiable sector of the town. It will be shown how the settlers were regarded with contempt on social grounds; contempt which was sufficient to constitute a barrier between them and natives of Cardiff.

Low social status is, however, only one factor which makes for the social separation of this particular group. A very potent force acting against the assimilation of the Catholic minority was religious hostility. As the following pages will show, the religious prejudice against the immigrants found expression in many ways throughout the development of the settlement. Sometimes the expression was subtle, often it was crude, now and then it was violent; its total effect was to strengthen the 'wall' around the newcomers.

These are the external factors which make for isolation. They are 'external' in the sense that they are hostile pressures exerted by the host society on the newcomers which made the latter feel it necessary to reduce their contacts with their social environment to the minimum possible. To these must be added internal factors—forces operating within the immigrant group itself—which were equally potent in producing isolation. There is, to begin with, the force of reaction within the group to the hostility from outside. This in itself was sufficient to drive the Catholics in upon themselves and to force a solidarity amongst them in the face of a 'common enemy'. But the force of reaction itself is not sufficient to explain the long period of separation which followed the establishment of the Catholic group in the first sixty years of the nineteenth century; no merely negative factor could do that. It is here that the two elements of religion and nationality become of particular importance. Common membership of the Catholic Church provided the immigrants with a unifying bond as well as a means of self-identification within the larger society and thus provided the potential for the building of a strong and institutionalised community life. This potential was realised largely through the presence of the Roman Catholic priests who attached themselves to the group and who provided the immigrants with the leadership necessary to build a communal life largely independent of the host society.

The Irish nationality of the immigrants played its part as an isolating force by moving the attention of Catholics from domestic politics to the tribulations of Ireland and its struggle for independence. The full implications of this are so important for Catholics in England and Wales generally that a full chapter—Chapter 6—has been devoted to them. The total effect of both these sets of factors—internal and external—has been the development of a pattern of life amongst Catholics which began in isolation and which has endured in isolation for over a century. At the present time the signs are that this situation is changing, and there is evidence to suggest *why* it is changing. It is now possible, also, to offer an analysis of the process of change and this is done particularly in Chapter 7.

Cardiff as a city is a product of the industrial developments which took place in South Wales during the nineteenth century. Throughout the eighteenth century Cardiff remained a small community containing approximately one thousand people and existing as the centre of the agricultural area of the Vale of Glamorgan. In common with many other small ports along the coast of South

*Table 2*

Total population of Cardiff, 1801–1951.

| Year | Population |
|------|-----------|
| 1801 | 1,870 |
| 1821 | 3,521 |
| 1841 | 10,077 |
| 1861 | 32,954 |
| 1881 | 82,761 |
| 1901 | 164,333 |
| 1921 | 200,184 |
| 1931 | 223,589 |
| 1951 | 243,632 |

N.B. No figures are available for 1941; the population for 1931 has been given in order to avoid having a gap of thirty years.

Wales, Cardiff engaged in the shipment of coal for sale in other parts of Britain and it was this activity which provided the key to its future development as a thriving industrial settlement. During the nineteenth century there was a progressive development of the coalfield which spread across the valleys of South Wales, and an outlet had to be found for the shipping of this coal not only to other parts of Britain but also to many countries abroad. It was to meet this need that Cardiff was developed. A canal was dug and a railway built to link the town with the coal-field, and a network of docks was constructed in the town itself to cope with the vessels needed for transporting the coal.

Work of this nature demanded an increasing amount of labour which could not be supplied by the small population of eighteenth-century Cardiff. The result was that there was a steady immigration of workmen from the surrounding counties of Wales and England and from the south-east counties of Ireland. These people settled in Cardiff and as commerce in general and the coal trade in particular flourished during the nineteenth century the town grew in size until in the middle of the twentieth century its population amounted to almost a quarter of a million. The above table demonstrates this growth.

It is interesting, also, to look very briefly at the occupations of the inhabitants of Cardiff at different times. It appears from the Cardiff Records that, at least until 1835, there was no class of merchants or manufacturers in the town. Until Cardiff began to be transformed by the industrial developments after the first quarter of the nineteenth century its occupational divisions remain fairly static. There were a small number of 'gentry' in the town—though the report to the Board of Health of 1850 takes pains to point out that it was not a town which 'gentlemen' would find attractive to live in—a number of yeomen farmers and small tradesmen—mercers, hatmakers, tobacconists, journeymen carpenters, etc.—and a labouring population made up of farmworkers and men connected with the slight activity in the port.

By 1851, however, the working population was beginning to reflect the increased activity in the town and was becoming more diversified, as the following table shows:

*Table 3*

Percentage of labour employed in different trades in Cardiff, 1851.

| | 1851 |
|---|---|
| Agriculture | 4·7% |
| Iron and Steel | 7·0% |
| Shipbuilding | 3·2% |
| Coal mining | 5·0% |
| Railway | 2·2% |

| | |
|---|---|
| Canal service | 2·5% |
| Building | 17·0% |
| Occupations connected with the sea (pilots, seamen, etc.) | 58·4% |

Table constructed from the census volumes, 1851.

The Irish immigrants, for reasons discussed later, were engaged mainly in the unskilled sectors of all these trades except agriculture and coal mining. In this they followed the general pattern outlined earlier in the study.

The examination of the Catholic community in Cardiff has been divided into two sections, the 'establishment' and the 'development'. In the period of establishment immigration was continuously rising and there was apparently no ordered community among the newcomers; in the period of development, immigration steadily declines and the group begins to take shape. The dividing date, 1861, is, of course, arbitrary, but it has been selected because in that year immigration from Ireland had reached its peak and because St. Peter's Church was opened—an event which symbolises the opening of an era in which the community enters a phase of rapid institutionalisation.

To determine the number of Catholics living in Cardiff before 1861 recourse has been had to two major source areas—the Government censuses and the parish records noted in the Diary of the Fathers of the Institute of Charity (Rosminians) who came to Cardiff in 1854. Government censuses show the number of people of Irish birth in Cardiff, while parish records show the number of Catholics. It has been felt justifiable, however, to combine the use of both of these because strong evidence exists to show that the Catholic population was practically one hundred per cent Irish in origin. At the beginning of the nineteenth century the native population of Cardiff was almost entirely non-Catholic; indeed, prior to 1822 there were only two Catholics known to reside in Cardiff, and one of these was an Irishman. On the other hand there were very few immigrants into Cardiff who may have come from countries where Catholicism was the prevailing religion. The census of 1851, for instance, indicates that there were 674 persons born in 'Foreign Parts' living in Cardiff; the particular 'Foreign Parts' in question are not specified.

## ESTABLISHMENT OF THE CATHOLIC SETTLEMENT IN CARDIFF, 1800–61[1]

In 1857 there was a note made in the Cardiff Diary of the Fathers of Charity, by the Rev. Fr. Signini, of a deposition by one of John Driscoll of Cardiff.[2] According to this deposition, there was only one Irishman known to reside in Cardiff prior to 1822—his name was James McLoughlin. About 1822, Jeremiah Mahony, who was still living in Mary Ann Street in 1857, John Donahue, who resided at Union Buildings (now Morgan Arcade) and John Driscoll, the deponent, came to settle in the town and in three or four years their number increased to a dozen.

Confirmation of John Driscoll's statement may be found in the register of St. John's. The first obviously Irish burial entries in the nineteenth century are 'John Barry of Tunnell Buildings, aged 6 months—on February 5th 1826', and 'Daniel Donahue of the Hayes, aged 2 years, 22nd December, 1826'. At the end of 1826 there were, according to the registers, the following Irish people living in Cardiff: Patrick Dogan or Duggan, Jerry Marney or Mahoney, Ann McLoughlin (possibly the widow of James McLoughlin, the first Irishman), Dennis Sullivan, the Barry family and the Donohue family. There is an increasing number of Irish names appearing in the Registers down to 1838, when it was no longer necessary for Catholics to marry in St. John's as well as before a priest (registrars were appointed in 1837). It may be noted that women came with the men, e.g. Mary Donahue, Mary Santry, Mary Hayes and Mary Begley are among those who either married Irishmen or signed the register as witnesses.

The Irish population increased steadily until in 1841 there were 1,200 persons on the register of St. David's. The reasons for this are to be found in the considerable work that was being done to

---

[1] Much of the material for this section is based on the relevant portion of my unpublished M.A. thesis, 'The Origin and Growth of the Irish Community in Cardiff' (University of Wales, 1959).

[2] Cardiff Diary of the Fathers of Charity.

develop Cardiff as a port for the export of coal from the South
Wales coal-field, and to serve the ironworks in the South Wales
valleys. The building of the Bute Dock occupied the middle years
of the 1830's and the works were completed in 1839. Similarly, the
Taff Vale Railway, which was built to link Cardiff with the coal-
fields, was completed in 1841. The demand for labour which these
schemes would produce accounts, then, for the increase in the Irish
population up to 1841. In the light of what has already been said of
the virtues of Irish labour for the heavy work involved in dock and
railway building, it is natural that employers should look to Ireland
to supply labourers, and the proximity of South Wales to the Cork
and Waterford areas of Ireland would make migration to Cardiff a
fairly simple matter.

After 1841 there is a decline in the numbers of the Irish in
Cardiff, caused, no doubt, by the completion of the Docks and
Railway, and by 1845 the figure had dropped to 900. From 1845,
however, there is a steady increase over the years: in 1848 there
were 2,300 on the register of St. David's, in 1850 there were 3,700
and in 1861 the numbers at St. David's and St. Peter's had reached
10,800. This influx can be attributed directly to the effects of the
Famine. As we shall see later, there is no doubt that the Irish who
streamed into Cardiff during the years 1848–51 in particular were
the victims of the disaster which had befallen their homeland, and
came in search of a refuge. In the years between 1851–5 there
was the added incentive of employment to bring the immigrants,
for during these years Cardiff Dock was being extended and in
1855 the East Bute Dock and Basin was completed.

## (i) *Social Status of the Immigrants: General Picture*

The social status of the Irish immigrants was, of course, directly
related to their occupations. G. C. Lewis reported that their work
was 'usually of the roughest, coarsest and most repulsive description, and requiring the least skill and practise'. They were, then, at
the bottom of the social scale, on a level with, or even below, the
poorest of the indigenous population. In Cardiff, in the early 1840's
before the post-Famine flood, a number of the Irish could be
described as 'mendicants'. The *Cardiff Advertiser and Merthyr*

*Guardian* reports cases of Irish seeking money from the courts to pay their fares home, but by 1842 the number of such cases was so high that the editor no longer felt it worth while to publish an account of them. The affairs of these 'gentry', he felt, were not, in any case, of sufficient value to merit the attention of his readers.

The Commissioner on Education in Wales noted that at that time, there was little permanent poverty in the town except among the Irish.[1] His opinion was supported by that of the Rev. Patrick Millea, the Catholic priest appointed to minister to the needs of the Irish Catholics in Cardiff, who stated that the numbers of his congregation were, with few exceptions, 'of the labouring class, and many of them the poorest of the poor'.[2] Further evidence of the social standing of the Irish can be gained from the evidence of the Superintending Inspector sent by the Government to report on the sanitary condition of Cardiff in 1849.[3] In his report, the Inspector deals, amongst other things, with the increase in the population of Cardiff which was taking place during the year under examination. The increase had led to many problems, particularly because, as he said:

'. . . the worst of these straggling accessions to the local popula-tion is, that they too generally consist of the most wretched members of the society from which they have, as it were, been cast forth—generally, in a starving condition, after already afflicted with disease, or carrying the seeds of it about with them.'[4]

In the Report is contained, also, evidence of the Superintendent of Police who spoke of the conditions existing in some of the areas of the town notorious for the unruly behaviour of the residents. Here there are references to inhabitants who are the 'lowest class of Irish', and a complaint that their activities 'call frequently for the interference of the police'.[5]

During the years 1846–9 there were epidemics of typhus and

---

[1] *Report of the Commission on the State of Education in Wales*, appendix, p. 366, vol. 1.
[2] *Ibid.*, pp. 371–2.
[3] *Report to the general board of health on the town of Cardiff, 1850.*
[4] *Ibid.*, p. 13.          [5] *Ibid.*, p. 40.

cholera in Cardiff. The main weight of the blame for these outbreaks was laid at the door of the Irish; the medical officer of the
Cardiff Union stated that the main cause of the increase in disease
was the 'immense invasion of Irish destitute labourers, navigators
and others, who had been brought over to this town by public
works.'[1] His assistant goes so far as to say that the majority of cases
of fever 'may be said to have been imported direct from Skibbereen
and Clonakilty'.[2]

It is not surprising, then, if these factors are taken into account,
that the inhabitants of Cardiff regarded the Irish settlement with
disfavour and considered its members as a class apart from and
inferior to the rest of the population of the town. Considerations
such as these would have prompted the author of the article which
appeared in the *Cardiff Advertiser and Merthyr Guardian* of the
last week in March 1850 to write, describing the celebrations of
St. Patrick's Day:

> 'We are accustomed to associate notions of filth, squalor and
> beggarly destitution with everything *Irish* from the large number
> of lazy, idle and wretched natives of the Sister Island who are
> continually crossing our paths . . .'

This attitude, which shows strongly not only in newspaper
comment at the time but also in official reports (which will be
considered later), was typical of the outlook of those townsmen
who were in a position of authority and influence and must have
served to relegate the Irish to a position of the social scale lower
than that of the most inferior of the native labouring class. The
latter, after all, had not brought 'Irish famine fever' with them
into the town, had not arrived 'bringing pestilence on their back,
famine in their stomachs'.[3] and had not arrived in such large
numbers seeking relief. The fact that the Irish were almost entirely
Catholics was not likely to endear them to the native inhabitants
either, and this was a further reason for the fact that the settlement
was considered as something apart.

---

[1] *Ibid.*, p. 44.                                    [2] *Ibid.*, p. 44.
[3] Government Inspector in Report (*op. cit.*), p. 41.

## (ii) *Class Division among the immigrants*

It would be an over-simplification of the picture, however, to leave it as one merely of a completely depressed body of refugees from the Famine. There were divisions among the Irish themselves. The members of the settlement who had arrived prior to the Famine contained among them persons of a different type from those who arrived in such great numbers after 1847. Evidence for this is to be found in many ways. The first settlers, i.e. those who came between 1822–47 were not all illiterate. The registers of St. John show that some of them, at least, were capable of reproducing signatures in very fair handwriting. They had, furthermore, a concern for education. The Rev. Patrick Millea, in the letter already cited, mentions the existence of a school which must have existed in the early 1840's at the latest. The school was held 'in a room or two in some back place only fit for cattle', yet the subjects taught included 'arithmetic, geography, English grammar, reading, writing, etc.', a not unambitious programme for the children of the poorer classes of that time. Before the building of the Chapel of St. David in 1842, centres of worship, admittedly small and unsatisfactory were set up, indicating that an attempt had been made to bring the Irish settlers in Cardiff into close contact with their religion, even though they were small in resources and could ill afford to rent premises and support a pastor.[1]

It was in the early forties, also, that the Ancient Order of Hibernians was formed.[2] The appearance of a branch of this national organisation in Cardiff at such an early date in the history of the settlement is of some significance. The Ancient Order of Hibernians was set up to encourage, through saving and insurance schemes, the virtues of thrift and concern for the future among its members; there must have been, then, Irishmen in Cardiff at that time who possessed these virtues so highly regarded by their fellow-townsmen and who, as a result, must have felt a gulf to exist between themselves and the new arrivals after 1847.

[1] See letter of Bishop Brown quoted in *Ordo*, 1843.

[2] The early records of the Cardiff branch of the Ancient Order of Hibernians have been lost, but the existence of the branch in the 1840's is indicated by the fact that by 1850 they were sufficiently organised to be able to hold St. Patrick's day celebrations.

These facts indicate that there was some attempt to organise the Irish settlement along sound lines, prior to the post-Famine influx and that there must have been a 'leader-class' among the Irish themselves. It is from among these men that the clergy, who were mainly responsible for the later organisation of the Irish community drew their initial lay support. Their existence was noticed, with some surprise, by the author of the article in the *Cardiff Advertiser and Merthyr Guardian*, March 1850, already quoted, who thought them worthy of special commendation. Nevertheless, their numbers were not sufficiently large to overcome the general attitude of the native population to the Irish; these exceptional individuals were obliged by the general attitude of their fellow-townsmen, even if they were not, in any case, naturally inclined to associate themselves with the general body of the Cardiff Irish. The results of this I hope to show later.

THE NATURE OF THE SETTLEMENT IN CARDIFF

(i) *Location*

In the first years of the settlement, i.e. between 1822–41, the Irish immigrants were spread throughout the poorer sections of the town—Tunnel Buildings, Union Buildings, the Hayes and Bute Street, being some of the addresses to be found in the registers of St. John's and St. David's. There was also a concentration of Irish, after 1841, in the area around St. David's Chapel, particularly in Stanley Street. With the influx after 1847 it is this latter area which became the centre of the settlement and, throughout the century, the Irish spread outwards from here.

The evidence which helps to locate the area of the settlement is to be found mainly in the *Report to the General Board of Health on Cardiff* (London, 1850), which has already been quoted, and in the *Annual Reports* of the Medical Officer of Health for Cardiff for the year 1853 and following.

The Report of 1850 shows Stanley Street to be occupied almost exclusively by Irish. Large concentrations of them were to be found in the streets adjacent to Stanley Street, Mary Anne Street, Love Lane, Little Frederick Street and David Street—while Landore Court, Kenton Court and Mill Lane also contained many of the immigrants. In 1850, then, the area of the settlement lay roughly between the Taff Vale Railway on the East and St. Mary Street on the West, while it was bounded by Ebenezer Street on the North and the South Wales Railway on the South. At this time, Newtown, which was to become, in the twenty years following 1850, the centre of the Irish population in Cardiff, consisted only of about 100 houses, but it was steadily developing.

The reports of the Medical Officer of Health for Cardiff, the earliest of which extant is for the year 1853, trace the spread of the Irish into Newtown. Newtown is the area of Cardiff which, at that time, lay immediately to the east of the Taff Vale Railway. It was thus within 100 yards of Stanley Street and the streets adjacent to it and was the natural area to which the Irish would move. In 1853 the streets of Newtown were improved (i.e. pitched and paved) and by 1854 a large number of the immigrants were living in the district. The reports for this year indicates that there were at least 1,500 Irish living in four streets in Newtown—Ellen Street, Pendoylan Street, William Street and Thomas Street.[1] In 1855 the majority of the houses were occupied as Irish lodging houses.[2]

It is difficult to estimate accurately the number of Irish living in the areas outlined above. It would appear, from the reports already mentioned, that most of the houses in the area were used as lodging houses and, therefore, had a varying number of occupants who stayed in them for varying lengths of time. Prior to 1850, no check was kept on the numbers who lived at any given time in these houses and so no accurate figures are available; after 1850, when an inspector, drawn from the police, was appointed to visit lodging houses, a maximum number of occupants was laid down for each house.[3] This regulation, however, applied only to *places registered* as lodging houses and, therefore, did not, by any means, cover all the residences where lodgers were taken in. The most reliable guide to the actual number living in the area then, are the estimates in the

[1] *Report of the medical officer of health, 1855*, p. 7.

[2] *Ibid.*, p. 9 of this Report indicates, also, that there were 'filthy Irish lodging-houses' in Kenton's Court, Union Buildings, Tunnell Buildings, Whitmore Lane and Love Lane.

[3] Report of the medical officer of health, 1855, mentions the fact that sanitary supervision is carried out, but the actual number permitted to occupy each house is not stated.

reports which are taken from the figures given by the landlords of the houses or by neighbours. From these can be gathered the facts that in 1849 in Stanley Street, there was an average of 25–30 persons residing in each house (in one house the number is estimated at 60); there were, at that time, 18 houses in Stanley Street, occupied almost solely by Irish and so the total number of people living in that street was between 450–540. There are no figures available for the two streets running parallel to Stanley Street, David Street and Mary Ann Street—or for the streets near these thoroughfares—Little Frederick Street and Love Lane. These streets were occupied by Irish, however, and David Street and Mary Ann Street possessed roughly the same number of houses as Stanley Street. The rooms of the houses in David Street and Mary Ann Street were bigger than their counterparts in Stanley Street. A fair estimate, then, of the numbers living in David Street and Mary Ann Street would be in the region of 1,000 persons altogether. Love Lane and Little Frederick Street between them possessed about 18 houses of the same size as those in David Street and so would probably have housed in the region of 500 persons.

In the immediate area of Stanley Street in 1849, then, there would have been living approximately 2,000 Irish. The bulk of the remainder of the settlement was located in Landore Court and Kenton Court. The evidence of the Superintendent of Police indicates that in Landore Court there were living nearly 500 people, almost all of them Irish; figures for Kenton Court are not given but it is likely that they would be similar to those for Landore Court. In 1850, then, as far as can be estimated with any degree of certainty, there were approximately 3,000 Irish concentrated into the area of the settlement around Stanley Street.

Between 1850–9 the Irish population increased to 8,900 and the settlement spread into the Tindal Street area of Newtown. The numbers in this area were increased not only by immigration but also by some movement of the Irish from Stanley Street.[1] In 1854 there were 1,525 persons living in the 5 streets grouped together off Tindal Street, the vast majority of them Irish. In Tindal Street

[1] Report of the medical officer of health for 1858 shows that by that year the number of residents of Stanley Street had dropped to 262.

itself there were 13 lodging houses. The same difficulty applies to estimating the number of the occupants of these houses as was encountered in dealing with Stanley Street and the adjacent area. No definite figures are available but in the 1855 report the medical officer of health estimated that the number of inmates in each house varied nightly from between 13–20 persons. Taking this as a rough guide there would be, in 1859, between 169–260 Irish living in the Tindal Street lodging houses. Added to this figure would be the 1,525 in the 5 streets mentioned above which gives a total of between 1,694 and 1,785 living in the Tindal Street area of Newtown.

The number of Irish living in the areas based on Stanley Street and Tindal Street in 1859 then, would be approximately 5,000. This figure is almost certain to be an under-estimate, however, for, although the medical officer kept a check on the houses registered as lodging houses, even these, as he ruefully admits in the reports of 1858 and 1860, took advantage of any occasion when an inspection was expected to be carried out, to increase the number of occupants. The actual number of Irish, then, who occupied the lodging houses was likely to be substantially higher than the estimate made.

In 1850 the type and quality of the houses built in Cardiff varied considerably. Those houses which were occupied by the gentry and the professional and merchant class and which lay in the area covered by Queen Street and Castle Street in the North and Ebenezer Street in the South were of as high quality as conditions permitted. The highest quality houses were, generally speaking, in the older part of the town, the newer houses, including those being built in 1850, being of inferior quality.[1] As a general rule, most of the houses built in the Stanley Street–Docks–Newtown area about 1850 were two- or four-roomed cottages. The acute housing shortage between 1840 and 1861 encouraged speculative building without any concern for the future comfort and conveniences of the occupants. In 1849 the Town Surveyor reported that 'houses of the lower class . . . are now commonly let before even the first

[1] *Report to the general board of health on the town of Cardiff* (London, 1850), *op. cit.*, p. 11.

stone is laid'. These houses were built 'without any regard to level or uniformity'[1] so that it was almost impossible to construct decent roads and pavements between them; in streets that had been paved, the floors of the houses were often below the level of the paving. The drainage problem created by such building will be considered in the next section. Some of these houses still stand today and confirm the impression gained from contemporary sources that the general standard of housing at the time was extremely low.

## (ii) *Living conditions of the immigrants before 1845*

The living standards of the Irish who came to settle in Cardiff between 1822 and 1845 mainly to work on the docks and the railway, were on a par with those of other workers in the town; they were poor, but there was little real suffering among them and they were able to maintain a higher standard of living than the flood of new immigrants who came between 1845 and 1861. In 1841 they numbered about 1,200, roughly 10 per cent of the total population of the town. Because of their relative insignificance in numbers and their general identity with other workers, information about the state of the Irish before 1845 is more difficult to find than after that date when the Irish problem came increasingly into the public eye. There are certain leads, however, which can be followed.

The fact that the immigrants' standard of living was not noticeably different from that of the general labouring class in 1841 is shown, first of all, by the areas they inhabited. As has already been noted, the Irish, at this time, were scattered throughout the poorer quarters of Cardiff—Tunnel Buildings, Union Buildings, the Hayes and Bute Street—and there was not a clearly defined 'Irish quarter' before 1845. There were, as I have mentioned in an earlier section, numbers of mendicant Irish who aroused the scorn of the local press, and *socially* the general body of Irish tended to be classed with these mendicants; but the fact that they may have been allocated by contemporaries to a social position beneath that of the labouring class does not necessarily prove that the living standards of the Irish who settled in Cardiff were inferior to those of the labouring class.

[1] *Ibid.*, comment of the Government Inspector, p. 16.

This point is emphasised by the concern of these early settlers for the education of their children. The *Report of the Commission on Education, 1847* lists five schools (excluding sunday schools) as existing in Cardiff at that date. Of these, one was a Catholic school catering for the Irish population. Fr. Millea's letter to the Commissioner mentions the existence of a school before 1847, so that the Irish were not behind their fellow-townsmen in providing for the needs of their children in this sphere at least.

Also of significance for this point is the existence of the thrift and insurance society already referred to and the fact that the Irish were able to maintain a priest, albeit very frugally, to minister to their spiritual needs. Bishop Brown, O.S.B., the first Roman Catholic Vicar Apostolic of the Welsh District, writing in 1841 states that the income of the missioner in Cardiff—the Rev. Patrick Millea—throughout that year varied between 5/- and 8/- per week.[1] He was entirely dependent for his livelihood upon the subscriptions of working men who, in 1841, had suffered from the cessation of work in the building of the Taff Vale Railway and the falling-off of employment at the iron works in Cardiff. The Bishop goes on to state that:

'. . . owing to the charity of Mrs. Eyre of Bath, and her son and executor, Thomas Eyre, Esq., a chapel had been commenced to replace the densely crowded floor of the cottage from which the window frame must be removed on Sundays in order that hundreds exposed to the weather in the roofless backyard, may discharge their religious duties.'[2]

[1] Letter of Bishop Brown quoted in *Ordo* 1843.

[2] *Ibid.*, the conditions revealed in this letter were not, of course, endured only by Catholics in Cardiff. In the town of Merthyr Tydfil—a thriving industrial town not far from Cardiff—conditions for priest and congregation were even more straitened than in Cardiff, as the following account will show:
'The very talented and zealous pastor of Merthyr Tydfil has under his care about 700 poor Irish, who are employed in the iron and coal works at Merthyr Tydfil and other places scattered at the distance of seven or eight miles around. He has no chapel, but says two Masses every Sunday; one at Merthyr, in a granary over a slaughter house, and the other at six miles distance (which he travels on foot) in a wash house. He has a school for about 50 poor children of both sexes, in a one-horse stable, about eight feet wide and sixteen feet long. His own dwelling is a workman's cottage, without a single article of decent furniture and often, it is feared, without a sufficiency of food . . .' (*Laity's Directory, 1840*, p. 32).

This new church, dedicated to St. David, was opened in October
1842.

These two institutions of church and school symbolised the
immigrants' claim to a position in the social structure of the town
at least equivalent to that of the labouring class; the existence of
the Ancient Order of Hibernians indicated that some, at least,
of the settlers aimed to improve their standard of living still
further.

### (iii) *Living conditions of the immigrants, 1845–61*

In the period 1845–61, that is during the years which saw the
influx of the Irish into Cardiff following the Famine, the living
conditions of the settlement sank very low. This was due mainly
to the condition of the immigrants when they left Ireland and the
conditions which confronted them when they reached Cardiff.
Enough has already been said to show that the majority of the
Irish who came to the town during the famine years, came ill-
equipped to begin a new life in a strange land. Many of them had
endured years of privation in Ireland and landed in South Wales
in a half-starved condition; many of them, also, were suffering
from diseases on their arrival and were not fit for work even if it
were available; few of them had the prospect of jobs to go to on
arrival. Some of the immigrants, in fact, went straight to the work-
house for relief before even taking up abode in Cardiff. In 1848, for
example, the Relieving Officer of Cardiff reported that several of
the orphan children given relief were those of Irish parents who
had died of 'Irish famine fever', after having been landed on the
neighbouring coast in a state of disease and starvation.[1]

The conditions which the immigrants found on their arrival in
Cardiff did little to suggest that they could improve on the living
standards they had experienced in Ireland. The root of the problem
lay in the shortage of housing and the poor sanitary conditions in
the town. The pressure on existing accommodation led to a rise in
the rents of those cottages which were available, so that the Town
Surveyor wrote, in 1849:

[1] *Report to the General Board of Health on the town of Cardiff* (London, 1850),
*op. cit.*, evidence of E. John, Relieving Officer of Cardiff, p. 47.

'The rents of the cottage property throughout the town is very high. The very lowest class of cottages—those in Stanley Street, for instance—which have only two rooms each, and the building of which would not have cost more than £40, let for £6 10s. a year; very inferior cottages let as high as £10 a year.'[1]

In 1857 the medical officer of health reported that houses in Newtown which had been created at a cost of between £105 and £110 were let, without difficulty, at from 5/6d to 6/- a week.

These factors brought about a tremendous increase in the number of lodging houses that existed in the town, and which were occupied very largely by the Irish immigrants. The rents of the cottages were so high that they were beyond the pockets of the majority of wage-earners and certainly were out of reach of the impoverished immigrants who arrived after 1845. It became a common practice, then, for Irishmen who perhaps had been in Cardiff for some years before 1845, to take over the tenancy of houses in the area of the Irish settlement and to take in their fellow-countrymen as lodgers. This enabled such tenants to provide the new immigrants with shelter of a sort; they were also able not only to meet the high rents but, in some cases, to make a substantial margin of profit.

The use of small dwellings as lodging houses was not sufficient to meet the needs of the time without chronic overcrowding. This produced serious results for, not only were the houses very small but they were also, in 1849, inadequately provided with drainage. These factors combined to bring the living conditions of the post-Famine immigrants down to a level below that of the lowest section of society in the town. An examination of conditions which existed in Stanley Street in 1849, conditions which were repeated through-out the rest of the area of the Irish settlement, will indicate the state in which the majority of the settlers who came between 1845–55 were obliged to live.[2]

---

[1] *Op. cit.*, evidence of Town Surveyor, p. 33.

[2] The information concerning conditions in Stanley Street is contained in the evidence submitted by the Superintendent of Police, the Town Surveyor and the assistant medical officer to the Government Inspector who prepared the Report on Cardiff to the General Board of Health quoted above.

In 1849 Stanley Street consisted of 18 houses, owned by a Mr. Wm. Stanley and a Mr. Wm. Evans. One end of the street had been built on and it had been partially pitched; the width of the street from house to house was 15 feet. The houses followed a common pattern, consisting of two rooms each, one above the other, with the exception of one house which had four rooms. The sanitation in each house was crude—they each possessed one privy which was housed in a small room opening directly on to the living room. The street itself was never scavengered.

The rents of these houses varied between 2/6d and 4/- a week, with the exception of one house (possibly the four-roomed one) rented by a John Bryant for 8/- a week. The houses varied slightly in dimensions: no. 1, for instance, possessed rooms 10' 0" long, 11' 0" wide and 7' 0" high; no. 5 had rooms 12' 2" × 11' 7", while the rooms in no. 15 measured 17' 3" × 17' 0" × 7' 10". The remainder came within the range between nos. 1 and 15.

The tenants of these houses were Irishmen some of whom, in 1849, had been there between seven and ten years. For example, no. 9 was rented by Michael Mahony who had lived there since 1842, no. 10 was rented by John Harrington who had been there since 1839 and no. 15 had been occupied by John Bryant since 1842. The tenants of the other houses included among their number Cornelius Driscoll (no. 6), Daniel Leary (no. 11), Jerry Collins (no. 12) and Michael Harrington, so there is no real need for the Inspector to note that the inhabitants were mainly Irish.

Each of the houses in Stanley Street was used as a lodging house. The tenants took in immigrants on either a permanent or a nightly basis, i.e. some of the lodgers lived, ate and slept in the houses and some came there at night merely to sleep. The majority of the immigrants, arriving as they did in a state of penury, were in no position to demand comfortable accommodation for themselves and their families even if they could have found it; they wished merely for shelter. The result was that in Stanley Street the houses were crammed far beyond their capacity with immigrants who were prepared to endure the most appalling living conditions in exchange for a roof over their heads.

The report of the Superintendent of Police (1849) gives a graphic account of the living conditions in Stanley Street. In no. 17, the lodging house kept by Michael Harrington, 54 persons were living, men, women and children. All these people lived, ate and slept in one room measuring 15′ 10″ × 17′ 2″ × 8′ 6″; as may be expected, the smell arising from the room was 'overpowering'. In one of the houses rented from William Evans there was, at the time the Superintendent made his visit, a woman who had been recently confined. She was in a room measuring 10′ 0″ square and in which there were three other beds. Three persons slept in each bed every night. 'The stench arising from these houses was like that from a foetid cesspool' (report, p. 35).

After quoting these examples, the Superintendent goes on to describe the conditions of other houses in Stanley Street. Most of the houses rented from William Evans each contained at least 14 persons who lived and slept there. The smallest number the Superintendent encountered in one of the houses was eight persons. To the number of people who lived in these houses, however, must be added the lodgers who came to sleep at night; there is no estimate given of the numbers of these. The overcrowding during the day-time, then, was considerably aggravated at night when the population of a house may have been more than doubled. In the lodging house already mentioned, rented by Michael Harrington, which had 54 inmates, many more came to sleep at night. The charge made for such lodgers was 3d, 4d or 6d for each adult, depending upon the accommodation; children were taken at halfprice.

The furniture in the houses was primitive in the extreme. In Michael Harrington's house there were no bedsteads at all, other than two 'stump' beds. All the lodgers, except the children, had to sleep on the ground; the children were given orange boxes or piles of shavings to sleep on in order to guard against the danger of being crushed by persons rolling on them in the night. Michael Harrington's was not an isolated case. John Bryant, who occupied no. 15, accommodated 36 persons in his house and took in nightly lodgers as well. There was no furniture of any description in the house other than 15 stump bedsteads placed close together. All the floor space and even the space under the beds was occupied by

l odgers who came at night and left in the morning. The inmates of
the house slept and ate in the same rooms.

The visits of the Superintendent to Stanley Street were made on
three occasions during April 1849. On his last visit the Superintendent noted that all the houses in Stanley Street contained the
'usual number' of occupants and every room was crowded. In
Michael Harrington's house a woman named Kitty Tyler had been
confined two days before in a crowded room. She had had no
medical assistance other than that of the woman of the house, and
at the time of the Superintendent's visit was on the floor of a room
occupied by about 20 other people.

It may be gathered from the Superintendent's report that similar
conditions to those existing in Stanley Street existed also in Mary
Ann Street, where the houses were sometimes crowded to suffoca-
tion, with full rooms and bedsteads placed close together. Landore
Court, also, witnessed similar conditions to those prevailing in
Stanley Street, the Superintendent stating: 'All the observations
I have made with regard to Stanley Street, as to the extreme overcrowding of the houses, apply equally here: they are inhabited
chiefly by the lowest class of Irish.'

The last word on this question of overcrowding in 1849 was said
by the assistant medical officer to the Cardiff Union. In his
evidence he stated that in Stanley Street, rooms were occupied
by relays of sleepers, some of whom were engaged on work during
the day and some in the night. In one bedroom, which measured
$12'\ 0'' \times 10'\ 0''$, there were 4 beds; in the day-time 6 men were
sleeping in three of the beds and at night these same beds were
occupied by another set of men. In Stanley Street it was the custom
for four or five families to sleep in one bedroom.

The reports of the medical officer of health indicate that the
problem of overcrowding among the Irish persisted until at least
1861.[1] The report of the year 1854 gives the total number of overcrowded lodging houses in the town as 279; there would be at least
16 occupants of each house, which gives a minimum of 4,464

[1] Report of the medical officer of health gives instances of overcrowding among
the Irish. The report also notes that the 'common lodging-houses in the town
required constant supervision, any relaxing of vigilance causing a relapse into
dirty and unhealthy conditions.

people living in overcrowded dwellings in that year. The causes of this lodging-house system were manifold but chief among them is ranked the constant flow of poor Irish immigrants who desired, first and foremost, a roof over their heads and who were 'indifferent to both comfort and cleanliness'. 'It would be difficult,' the report claims, 'to overstate the evil effects on the sanitary condition of this town, arising from this single cause.'[1]

The report for the year 1855 deals with the question of over-crowding among the Irish at Newtown. As has already been noted, the rents for the houses in Newtown had reached a high level at this time, due to the demand for accommodation; as a result of this, the tenant of the house, when called upon to meet a rent of between 5/6d–6/- a week out of a weekly wage in the region of 12/- a week, occupied one room of the house himself and sub-let the others at a rent of between 1/6d and 2/6d a week. The sub-tenants themselves frequently took in lodgers and, as a result, it was quite common to find 4–6 beds in one room, some occupied by adults and some by married couples. Two and, in some cases, three families with children were occupying the same room, staying there night and day.

These conditions had not improved much by 1857; the demand for accommodation was still so great that the abuses described were still in evidence, particularly in the Newtown area.[2] Houses were often let before the ground around them was paved or drained adequately and, consequently, filth accumulated rapidly. The following table illustrates the conditions complained of by the medical officer. The streets mentioned, with the exception of the last three, are all in the Newtown area. It was becoming common, however, for official reports to include Little Frederick Street, Stanley Street, Whitmore Lane and the streets adjoining in New-town and they were, in fact, as far as type of housing, occupants and location were concerned, part of the Newtown area, being separated from it only by the Taff Vale Railway line.

Bearing in mind the fact that the majority of these houses were merely 2- or 4-roomed cottages, the extent to which they were

---

[1] Report of the medical officer of health, 1854, p. 5.
[2] Report of the medical officer of health, 1858, p. 5.

overcrowded becomes obvious. It must also be remembered that whenever supervision of these houses was relaxed for a short period the number of occupants rose steeply.

The living conditions of the Irish were made considerably worse by the poor sanitary conditions of the houses they occupied. In Stanley Street, for example, the Town Surveyor stated, in 1849, that there were people sleeping in some rooms 'in which the most offensive privies are placed. These people all lie within 18 inches of the drain—and separated from it only by a rough wall.'[1] The

*Table 4:* Overcrowded houses: Stanley Street and Newtown Area.[2]

| Street | No. of houses with lodgers | No. of inmates | Average no. in each house | Greatest no. in one house |
|---|---|---|---|---|
| Pendoylan Street | 25 | 383 | $13\frac{1}{2}$ | 20 |
| Thomas Street | 28 | 366 | $13\frac{1}{2}$ | 23 |
| William Street | 32 | 522 | $16\frac{1}{2}$ | 26 |
| Ellen Street | 30 | 463 | $15\frac{1}{2}$ | 24 |
| Tyndal Street | 13 | 190 | $14\frac{1}{2}$ | 20 |
| Herbert Street | 6 | 130 | $21\frac{1}{2}$ | 23 |
| East Street | 14 | 181 | 13 | 20 |
| Little Frederick Street | 7 | 104 | 15 | 12* |
| Stanley Street | 29 | 262 | 9 | 13 |
| Whitmore Lane | 27 | 286 | $10\frac{1}{2}$ | 17 |

* 12 is the figure given in the Report. Obviously, as the average number is 15 then '12' must be inaccurate and is probably a misprint for 22.

owner of some of the houses in this street—Mr. William Stanley—himself reported that in one house the hole of the privy had been stopped up and the seat 'made to serve as a pillow to a bed upon which some persons slept.'[3]

Further evidence on this point is supplied by the report of the

[1] *Report to the General Board of Health on the town of Cardiff* (London, 1850), *op. cit.*, p. 33.
[2] *Ibid.*, p. 7.
[3] *Ibid.*, p. 33.

Superintendent of Police.[1] Most of the rooms in Stanley Street, he said, were without ventilation as they lacked both back windows and back doors. The street itself was never cleaned so that in front of the houses there were heaps of decaying refuse which had been thrown out by the inmates themselves and which gave off a strong and offensive odour. The indoor sanitation of the houses was practically non-existent, the privies in most of them being stopped up and, in some cases, overflowing. In many cases the Superintendent refers to powerful smells coming from the houses, caused by lack of ventilation, stagnant water lying in the unpaved areas at the back of the houses and inefficient sanitation.

These conditions were not restricted to Stanley Street, Landore Court also suffered from primitive sanitary conditions. The Court led out of St. Mary Street by a narrow passage and was not a thoroughfare.[2] It was constructed on an irregular plot of ground measuring approximately 160′ 0″ long and 120′ 0″ wide, and was closely built up on three sides. In order that no space was wasted, a middle row ran down the centre between the two side rows. The passageway through the court was about 15′ 0″ broad, narrowing in some places to about 10′ 0″. There was no backlet to any of the houses, except to those in the centre plot; these opened into a court of irregular shape ranging from 6′ 0″ to 12′ 0″ or 15′ 0″ wide. In the court there were 27 houses in all, generally consisting of two rooms each, one above the other. These houses held, in total, nearly 500 people.

The sanitation was primitive. Some of the houses possessed closets, but nos. 1 to 6 were obliged to share two privies in front of nos. 1 and 2. There was, in addition, a public privy at the bottom of the court, open and without any form of covering. This latter became a depository of all kinds of filth as the contents of other privies and of the cesspools were occasionally dumped into it. There was no pump or water supply of any description in the court, and the inhabitants had to bring all the water they used from a pump in St. Mary Street.

Periodic outbreaks of typhus and cholera, diseases which are the natural result of such living conditions, added to the sufferings of

[1] *Ibid.*, pp. 39–40.            [2] *Ibid.*, pp. 35–7.

80

the immigrants. Epidemics were prevalent in Cardiff during the years 1846–9. Typhus fever broke out in the spring of 1847 and the outbreak lasted until the spring of 1848.[1] During that time the assistant medical officer to the Cardiff Union attended 283 cases of typhus in their own homes.

The disease gained a stronger hold in some areas than others and it was particularly virulent in the centre of the Irish settlement— Stanley Street, Love Lane, Whitmore Lane and Little Frederick Street. Between them these streets provided 122 cases of fever—over 40 per cent of the total—with 75 in Stanley Street, 8 in Love Lane, 25 in Whitmore Lane and 14 in Little Frederick Street. The drainage in these streets was of 'the worst description' and Stanley Street itself was sometimes almost impassable due to 'the quantities of veritable refuse and other noxious matters covering its surface.'[2] David Street, although it was surrounded by the other streets mentioned above, had only one case of typhus; this was due to the fact that David Street was broader than the neighbouring thorough-fares and its houses were less overcrowded and better and more cleanly kept than those in Stanley Street.

Outbreaks of cholera accompanied the epidemics of typhus fever. The area worst affected by cholera was identical with that for typhus and for the same reasons—overcrowding and bad sanitation.[3] In 1847 Stanley Street had 26 cases of cholera, Love Lane 7, Little Frederick Street 10 and David Street 8: there were very few cases in houses that were not overcrowded. In one house in Stanley Street which the medical officer visited during the epidemic of 1847 there were 43 persons, all of whom resided there permanently. The house had 4 rooms; five of the occupants had typhus. This example was repeated throughout the street. In no. 9, for example, a two-roomed house occupied by James Mahony, there were eight cases of cholera, six of which ended in death. The bodies were buried as soon as possible after death but, at one time, there were three corpses in the upstairs room. Landore Court did not escape the visitation of 1847; in that year there were 48 cases of typhus among the residents.

---

[1] *Ibid.*, evidence of the assistant medical officer to the Cardiff Union.
[2] *Ibid.*, p. 42.                              [3] *Ibid.*, p. 43.

There were many cases of fever among the Irish, however, which were not directly attributable to the conditions in which they lived but which had their root in the conditions in which the immigrants existed before they arrived in Cardiff. At the time of the outbreak of 1847, 186 cases of typhus fever, in addition to the 283 cases already mentioned, were admitted into a temporary hospital which had been set up on the outskirts of the town, 61 of these cases ended in death, and the medical officer comments that:

'This large proportion of mortality is to be accounted for by the circumstances of nearly all the cases being those of Irish, suffering from fever at the time of landing, and in a half-famished state, immediately going to the hospital.'[1]

The medical officer adds the comment already quoted in an earlier section: 'The cases in fact may be said to have been imported direct from Skibbereen and Clonakilty.'

By 1854 the measures which had been taken to improve the sanitation in the town had reduced the danger of death through cholera and typhus, e.g. in 1849 the outbreak had resulted in 347 deaths through cholera, while in 1854 there were 175 deaths.[2] Supervision of certain streets was now being carried out and the report of the medical officer of health for 1854 includes a table showing how this supervision had been effective in improving the living conditions of the occupants and curtailing the incidence of disease. The effect of the supervision was emphasised by the fact that there was no improvement in conditions in those streets which did not come under the control of the authorities. The two tables which follow show streets which are in or near the centre of the Irish settlement.

In Table 5 the section of seven streets had suffered severely from the outbreak of 1849, with a total of 93 deaths from cholera. At the time the houses were grossly overcrowded with 'labourers, indigent and mendicant Irish', and the majority were in a filthy condition, with no ventilation or water. Since 1849, the Common Lodging House Act had been brought into operation and, although the

[1] *Ibid.*, p. 44.
[2] Report of the medical officer of health, 1855.

houses were still occupied by the same type of person, they were
no longer overcrowded to the same degree. The rooms were cleaned
and lime-washed at regular intervals and an inspector visited them
daily to see if they were kept in proper order. Consequently the
deaths from contagious diseases dropped sharply down to 10 in
1854—and the health of the inhabitants was greatly improved. The
town authorities had not been able to apply the Common Lodging
House Act to the streets mentioned in Table 3; as a result, these
streets showed little or no improvement in their conditions and the
death rate from cholera only dropped from 27 in 1849 to 24 in 1854.

The general improvement in conditions continued throughout
the 1850's. In 1856 there was no fatal fever case in the Irish settlement—Newtown, Stanley Street, Landore Court—even though
there was still overcrowding in Newtown among the Irish. This

*Table 5:* Streets over which sanitary supervision had been adopted.[1]

| Street | Cases of cholera 1849 | Cases of cholera 1854 |
|---|---|---|
| Kenton's Court | 13 | 0 |
| Landore Court | 12 | 2 |
| Stanley Street | 19 | 1 |
| Love Lane | 8 | 4 |
| Whitmore Lane | 17 | 1 |
| Mary Ann Street | 12 | 2 |
| David Street | 12 | 0 |

*Table 6:* Streets not supervised.

| Street | Fatal cases of cholera: 1849 | Fatal cases of cholera: 1854 |
|---|---|---|
| Millicent Street | 18 | 16 |
| Bridge Street | 5 | 5 |
| Great Frederick Street | 4 | 3 |

[1] Tables 5 and 6 are taken from the report of the medical officer of health,
1855, p. 15.

improvement was due almost entirely to strict and regular supervision by an inspector of the lodging houses. Immediately this supervision was relaxed, however, the lodging houses relapsed into their previous conditions. In spite of this the medical officer of health was able to report in 1860 that, due to the general improvement in the conditions existing in the lodging houses 'Strumous ophthalmy, at one time a frequent disease among the Irish residents of this town, is now of rare occurance.'

### (iv) *Effects of these living conditions on the immigrants*

The living conditions which have been discussed had not only a deleterious effect upon the health of the Irish but also affected their living standards generally. The complete lack of privacy in the lodging houses, for one thing, must have affected their self-respect and sense of propriety in personal behaviour. The bulk of the immigrants were probably members of large families who had lived in cramped conditions in their homes in Ireland. They would not be strangers to overcrowding and would be likely to demand less in the way of living space than persons with a different background. Their distressed state would also induce them to accept, probably with gratitude, living conditions which would not have been tolerated by others who had not experienced the effects of the Famine.

Nevertheless the close mixing of men, women and children in these lodging houses outraged the susceptibilities of contemporary observers, and the apparent flouting of the conventional moral standards governing behaviour in the presence of the opposite sex by the occupants led to severe censure by local officials. The Superintendent of Police, in his report of 1849 dealing with Stanley Street, notes that in no. 15 the behaviour of the occupants left much to be desired in this respect. 'Not the slightest regard is paid to decency, the women being nearly naked in the presence of the men and children.'[1]

The medical officer of health was much concerned over this question of the moral standards of the immigrants living in the lodging houses, and in the report of 1861 he quotes several

---

[1] *Report to the General Board of Health on the town of Cardiff* (London, 1850), evidence of Superintendent of Police, p. 36.

examples to show the state in which the Irish lived. In no. 10
Love Lane, for instance, a house kept by Michael Donovan, a
man, his wife and two single men were occupying one bedroom;
in no. 3 Landore Court, kept by Dennis Dowling, two single men,
a man, his wife and two children occupied the same room.[1] Similar
conditions existed in houses in Rodney Street and Mill Lane,
which the medical officer quotes as examples. He concludes by
saying, rather plaintively:

> 'I have argued with these poor creatures on the gross want of
> decency and propriety in living in this uncivilised way. They do
> not appear aware of doing wrong: they consider it but as a
> natural consequence of having to pay so much for rent—this
> preventing them having greater accommodation: and they seem
> astonished you should imply evil consequences resulting from
> such a mode of living.'[2]

This quotation speaks eloquently of the great gulf in outlook and
accepted standards of behaviour which existed between such
persons as the medical officer and the newly arrived immigrants.
To the medical officer such a close mixing of the sexes showed a
'gross want of decency' and was 'uncivilised'. To the immigrant,
these questions were not of the first importance, or, at least, not as
the medical officer understood them. They were concerned
primarily with food and shelter, and conventional standards of
behaviour—conventional, that is, for the middle class of the people
among whom they had settled—were of minor importance compared with the achievement of the basic necessities of life. Under
these circumstances it is hardly surprising that they were
'astonished' at the implication of evil consequences from such a
manner of living: such consequences would never have been given
thought when the task of starting a new life in a completely strange
environment was being undertaken.

I have already said that communal living within one's own
family, with small dwellings shared by large numbers, must have
been the experience of most of the immigrants when they were

---

[1] Report of the medical officer of health, 1861, p. 16.
[2] *Ibid.*, p. 17.

living in Ireland on the land. They were thus easily satisfied as to living conditions and could not have expected much more privacy than they achieved in the lodging houses. There was little prospects then, of the scope of the immigrants' ambitions being raised and of a serious effort on the part of the majority to improve their living standards. To a person accustomed to such conditions, the prospect of being the sole occupier of a complete house, however humble, must have represented the goal of all effort. For many of the immigrants even this first step must have seemed one far too large for them to take.

That their manner of living affected nearly every aspect of the immigrants' life is illustrated, also, by one other aspect of the settlement in its early years, i.e. the frequency of 'early marriage' among the members of the Irish community and the consequent economic effects.

In the first forty years of the nineteenth century, early marriages, i.e. between persons in their late teens and early twenties, had become increasingly common in Ireland itself.[1] The main reason for this was that as there was a general shortage of land and little prospect of the sons of a family, other than the first-born, ever acquiring a share in the land of the father and thus gaining the opportunity of building up a flourishing holding, there was little incentive for such young men to put off marriage until they had secured a firm economic position. There was little likelihood of much improvement in their financial position and so little point in postponing a contemplated marriage. There was some tradition, then, to influence the outlook of immigrants on this matter. Cramped housing conditions, resulting in a close mingling of the sexes, encouraged this tendency for early marriage among the settlers in Cardiff. The result was increased economic hardship brought about by the arrival of children and, in its turn, a perpetuation of the problem of overcrowded living conditions. The children of such marriages themselves suffered due to the inability of the

---

[1] *Report on Emigration and other Population Problems, op. cit.*, table 56, p. 71. In 1841 the proportion of married exceeded the proportion of single in both sexes. The position has changed radically since 1841. Table 57 in the same report shows that in 1841 57·7 per cent of males and 72 per cent of females in the 25–34 age-group were married.

parents to provide them with adequate care and attention. This was reflected in the infant mortality rate among the Irish in Cardiff. In 1853 the infant mortality rate for the whole of Cardiff was one in three.[1] This compared very unfavourably with other parts of the country, e.g. the rate was one in five in London and one in eight in 'country districts'.[2]

The medical officer of health considered that the lodging-house system was the main cause of this high infant mortality rate. The majority of infant deaths occurred in the localities occupied by the Irish poor and were due to the mode of life of the Irish who occupied the lodging houses. In these houses:

'The sexes live and occupy the same rooms indiscriminately, hence early marriage and illegitimate births. Accustomed from a tender age to all kinds of privations, with no regard to comfort and decency, such people are little restrained by a sense of providence. A marriage of improvidence is with them the *rule*— a marriage of providence the *exception*. Their own *constitutions*, sapped by constant exposure to the vitiated atmosphere of their own crowded hovels, the weakly offspring, exposed to every influence such an atmosphere can engender, with little parental care, has feeble tenacity of life; the germs of scrofula develop their existence in the forms of strophy, mesenteric disease, hydrocephalus and convulsions, or, if it passes on for a short time beyond this period, the stunted, ricketty form of the Irish mendicant, testifies the hard battle it had to fight, ere consumption closes its miserable existence.'[3]

These facts paint a grim picture of the nature of the Irish settlement in the years between 1845 and 1861. There are, however, other aspects which must be considered if a true assessment of the community in its early years of life is to be reached. The impression gained from contemporary sources is one of a group of persons living generally in squalor, accepting conditions which no native of the town would have tolerated, possessing nothing other than

---

[1] Report of the medical officer of health, 1854, p. 3.
[2] *Ibid.*
[3] *Ibid.*

'heaps of rags, bones, salt-fish, rotten potatoes and other things',[1] and having standards of living which were below those of the community into which they had come.

### (v) *Other aspects of the community prior to 1861.*
### *Influence of 'superior' members of the community*

These conditions were not true of all the Irish, however, for there was, as has been seen, a small section of the community composed mainly of immigrants from the pre-Famine years, whose standards of living were on a par with those of the labouring classes generally in the town and who aimed to achieve a real status in the community. The influence of this section upon their less able or less fortunate countrymen was already being felt before 1861. These 'superior' Irish looked for their leadership to the clergy appointed by the Catholic Church to attend to their spiritual welfare and, as will become increasingly obvious, such leadership extended into almost every aspect of the life of the immigrants, covering not only religious practice but also education, social activities and relief of the destitute. It is interesting to note that the fact that the living conditions of this particular section of the immigrants were of a higher standard than their fellow-settlers was not sufficient to integrate them with their non-Catholic, non-Irish neighbours. This throws more light on the importance of the two remaining factors of religion and nationality as impediments to assimilation.

### *Education*

A start was made to provide educational facilities for the immigrants prior to 1850. Mention has already been made of the school opened by the Rev. Patrick Millea in David Street in 1847 and reported upon by the Commissioner on Education. The schoolroom is described in the report as measuring 40' × 19' and possessing an 'open roof, three good-sized windows, four skylights, two fireplaces, and a bricked floor'. There was a dwelling-house attached to the school and 'sufficient' outbuildings, the whole structure being held on a lease for 999 years.[2] The school was

---

[1] *Report to the General Board of Health on the town of Cardiff* (London, 1850), p. 36.  [2] Report on education, *op. cit.*, p. 371.

opened at a time when the flood of destitute Irish had been reaching Cardiff for about two years and it is reasonable to suppose that
the financial support necessary to build the school came from the
more firmly established members of the community (there is no
mention in Fr. Millea's report on the school of any one substantial
benefactor).

Fr. Millea had a considerable struggle to persuade the majority
of the settlers that education was beneficial for their children,
particularly when the parents discovered that they would have to
pay for it. Out of the 220 boys and girls who, in 1847, were of
school age, not more than eighty or ninety attended the school
regularly. The parents of these

> 'complained that they were not well able to pay for their
> children's schooling. The highest sum charged was four pence
> per week; this was done in order to leave the parents no cause
> for complaining, yet they considered it too much for their means;
> hence we may conclude that the greater part of the children of
> my congregation would want a gratuitous education.'[1]

Economic factors forced many parents to send the young
members of the family out to work at the earliest possible age
and they thus looked upon time spent at school beyond that age
as time wasted. They felt that 'if their children can read, that is
enough—they should thank providence and be satisfied—that
should be the *ne plus ultra*.'[2] By patient effort, however, the school
attendance was improved until the premises had to be extensively
enlarged in 1856, by which time the Irish population had increased
eight-fold. As the settlement grew after 1860 many more schools
were opened, through the agency of the clergy, in other parts of
Cardiff, but it took many years to eradicate the impression from the
minds of many of the Irish that education beyond the elementary
stage was a luxury only to be afforded by those who had no need to
engage in more productive tasks.

## Social activities

Some organisation was also attempted of the social activities of
the settlement, and here, again, the lead came from the clergy. The

[1] *Ibid.*, pp. 371–2.                                        [2] *Ibid.*

mode of life of the Irish severely limited the scope for recreation, and for many of them their only release from the realities of their existence was to be found in the taverns. Consequently, drunkenness reached serious proportions and became a matter of concern for the clergy, particularly at times like Christmas, when it became more prevalent. Eventually, in 1859, the Rev. Father Richardson visited Cardiff from Newport on 17 and 18 December, in order to establish an 'Association for the Suppression of Drunkenness'.[1] This association had only a limited effect, however, for it was necessary for further measures to be taken at different stages during the next twenty years.

Efforts were made to provide opportunities for the members of the community to spend their leisure hours in a more constructive and rewarding fashion than by merely frequenting the taverns. It was felt that the best way of doing this was to provide a means by which the members of the settlement could undertake activities in common. Thus in February 1859, the Rev. Brother Colton, a member of the Institute of Charity which had by now taken over the care of the Cardiff mission, came to Cardiff and founded a night school at which he taught.[2] No record exists of the number of students who attended these classes, and so no reliable estimate can be made of the appeal which they may have had to the immigrants. In order to influence as wide a section of the Irish as was possible, Brother Colton also formed a drum and fife band, an organisation which would be very familiar to the immigrants, and which would provide them with a link with their homeland. Again, no records of this band are in existence, but the tradition established in Cardiff in 1859 lasted for eighty years—an Irish drum and fife band existed in Cardiff until 1939.

These attempts to provide some organised social activity within the settlement, though small and probably short-lived,[3] set the patterns for the developments which were to take place in this sphere of activity during the latter half of the nineteenth century and the first quarter of the twentieth century. They are thus

---

[1] Cardiff Diary of the Fathers of Charity, 17 December, 1859.
[2] *Ibid.*
[3] Brother Colton left Cardiff the following year (see Cardiff Diary).

important as forerunners of activities which were to stamp the Irish settlement with characteristics which were to give them a sense of communal interest, and to mark them off from other sections of the population of Cardiff.

## Religious practice

The emphasis on the part played by the clergy in the leadership of the settlement leads on to the question of the religious practice of the members of the Irish community in Cardiff. It is difficult to estimate the precise degree of fervour with which any body of people practise their professed religion. It would be unwise to deduce from the fact that the clergy held a position of high prestige in the community the fact that the Irish were therefore punctilious in the discharge of their religious duties. They had come from a country where the Catholic Church played a major role in the life of the peasantry, influencing their whole mode of living. The parish priest was a figure of considerable importance in his area, for he was the people's acknowledged leader not only in spiritual affairs, but also in social and, often, political matters.[1] This state of affairs was inevitable in a society where community life was based on the parish, and where the priest, by virtue of his training, possessed educational standards well above those of his flock. A tradition had grown up among the Irish, in which the priest, by virtue first of his vocation, but also of his reputation as a man of wisdom and learning, occupied a position of dominating influence in the local community.

In these circumstances, it is possible that a proportion of the Irish community in Cardiff would accept the leadership of the clergy without necessarily being particularly fervent in their own personal religious beliefs, and consequently without being over-scrupulous about the practice of those beliefs. There are two indications which can lead to a rough assessment of the religious practice of the immigrants between the years 1841–61. Father Millea, in his report to the Commissioner on Education, notes that there was

[1] It is interesting to note that the influence of the clergy was not sufficient to prevent outbreaks of violence inspired by Fenianism in Ireland itself, but was almost completely successful in destroying elements of Fenianism in Cardiff among the Irish.

a Sunday school in existence 'where the children are instructed in the Catechism and their moral duties.'[1] Of the 220 children of school age, about 170 attended this Sunday school—over twice as many as went to the ordinary day school. This high proportion of

*Table 7:* Religious practice among the Irish in Cardiff, 1841–61.

| Year | Total Catholic population (taken from register of St David's) | Easter duties | Percentage of total |
|---|---|---|---|
| 1841 | 1,200 | 114 | 9·5 |
| 1842 | 1,100 | (No figures for these | |
| 1843 | 800 | two years) | |
| 1844 | 1,000 | 382 | 38·2 |
| 1845 | 1,100 | 270 | 24·5 |
| 1846 | 900 | 422 | 46·8 |
| 1847 | 1,000 | 500 | 50·0 |
| 1848 | 2,300 | 500 | 21·7 |
| 1849 | 2,600 | 530 | 20·3 |
| 1850 | 3,700 | 720 | 19·4 |
| 1851 | 4,000 | 960 | 24·0 |
| 1852 | 4,700 | 850 | 18·08 |
| 1853 | 6,000 | 950 | 15·8 |
| 1854 | 5,600 | 1,300 | 23·2 |
| 1855 | 6,600 | 1,550 | 23·4 |
| 1856 | 8,900 | 2,050 | 23·03 |
| 1857 | 8,900 | 2,100 | 23·5 |
| 1858 | 8,900 | 2,100 | 23·5 |
| 1859 | | (No figures given for this year) | |
| 1860 | 9,500 | 2,200 | 23·14 |
| 1861 | 9,800 | 2,500 | 25·5 |

attendance indicates that the majority of parents among the Irish were sufficiently conscientious about their religious duties to ensure, in 1846, that their children had a sound grounding in the basic beliefs of their Faith.

[1] Report on education, *op. cit.*, pp. 371–2.

The most common measurement by the clergy of religious practice among Catholics is attendance at 'Easter duties'. Catholics are obliged, under pain of serious sin, to receive the sacraments of penance and communion at least once a year; these duties must be fulfilled during a period falling between Ash Wednesday and one of the Sundays between Easter Sunday and the Sunday following Whit Sunday[1]—hence the term 'Easter duties'. The Cardiff Diary of the Institute of Charity contains the number of people who, between 1841–61, received the required sacraments during the allotted period of the year, and thus gives some indication of the number of Catholics who were fulfilling the minimum duties for membership of the Church.[2] The above table shows the figures for the period 1841–61.

There are certain factors to be borne in mind before any deduction is made from these figures. The number who made their Easter duties would all be persons over the age of 13 years: no children under that age, at that time, were required to fulfil the obligation.[3] There must also have been a proportion of sick or elderly persons who would have been unable to receive the sacraments. These two groups, of children under thirteen years of age, and the sick and aged, must be deducted from the totals of each year; consequently the percentages for each year would be proportionately higher. On the other hand, no details are given in the Diary of the method employed to arrive at the total of those who fulfilled the Easter duties.

The most common method nowadays is to count the actual number who receive the sacrament of penance during the period, and it is probable that this was also the method adopted during the middle years of the nineteenth century. The danger of double-counting (i.e. persons who received the sacrament of penance more than once during the allotted time) did not arise, because the penitent has always stated the length of time since his last con-

---

[1] The period during which a Catholic is obliged to receive the two sacraments mentioned has changed during the last hundred years. The starting point, Ash Wednesday, has remained constant but the end of the stipulated time has varied between Low Sunday and the Sunday following Whit-Sunday.

[2] These figures are taken from a note made by the Rev. Father Signini in the Cardiff Diary of the Fathers of Charity, 10 January 1864.

[3] The minimum age is now seven years.

fession. Lacking other evidence, however, the figures must still be treated with some reservation.

The table shows a very low percentage of the population fulfilling their duties in 1841, with a considerable increase in 1844 which is maintained, with the exception of 1845, until 1847, when the peak figure of 50 per cent is reached. From 1847 there is a sharp drop down to 21·7 in 1848, and this decline continues steadily, reaching 15·8 per cent in 1853. In 1854, the figure rises to 23·2 per cent, and remains remarkably constant until 1861 when it rises once more to 25·5 per cent.

The cause of this rise and fall can be found in the conditions which existed in the settlement during the years shown. The very low figure of 1841 is accounted for by the fact that it was only in that year that a priest was permanently based in Cardiff, to minister to the spiritual needs of the Catholics there. The early settlers had to depend upon the sporadic visits of a missioner from Dowlais or from Newport; if one was unavailable, they had to walk to Newport to attend Mass. During this period (1822–41) it is hardly surprising that, as the figures indicate, religious practice had declined among the Irish in Cardiff.

In 1842 the chapel of St. David's was opened and so a permanent centre of worship was now available. This, combined with the energetic efforts of Father Millea, accounts for the revival of religious practice up until the year 1847. Between 1847–8 the Catholic population of the town more than doubled, due to the influx of Irish after the Famine, and a decline followed. The one resident priest had been able to cope successfully with a community which was more or less static, but this sudden tremendous increase in his flock made the task of ensuring regular Church attendance extremely difficult. The problems were increased by the fact that the majority of the newcomers were destitute, living in appalling conditions and concerned primarily with the needs of food and shelter. As the numbers of immigrants grew during the years, so these problems became more pressing until, in 1853, the percentage of those actively practising their religion had dropped to 15·8.

The position was complicated by the fact that, between the

departure of Father Millea in 1849 and the arrival of the Institute of Charity in 1854, the Cardiff mission was served by priests who were able to stay only for short periods before being recalled to duties elsewhere. As a result, it was not until the appointment, in 1854, of another priest who was a member of the Institute of Charity, once more permanently resident in Cardiff, that measures could be taken to revive the religious practice of the community.

By 1855 the percentage had reached 23·2 and it remained at this figure, with only slight variations, until the influx of Irish immigrants reached its peak in 1861. When all allowances have been made for conditions which existed in the settlement, the point still emerges that, although the Irish were prepared to afford respect and prestige to the clergy they were not, as a body, particularly conscientious in the practice of their religion. This seems to emphasise the point already made—that the Church exercised considerable influence over the Irish quite apart from their own individual piety—and to indicate that membership of the Church and respect for its representatives was as much a social as a religious necessity for the immigrants.[1] The feeling of belonging, even precariously, to a community such as the Church with recognised leaders gave the immigrants some status and security which they sorely needed in the circumstances in which they lived. Common membership of the Church also acted as a binding-force among the community; such membership was, in fact, an integral part of their nationality as Irishmen. The Church had for centuries played such a major role in the life of Ireland that for an Irishman of the peasant class to lose his Catholicism was almost equivalent to losing his nationality.

*Summary*

The years in which the Cardiff Irish community was founded show a many sided picture. There was, at first, the thin trickle of immigrants who arrived during the years 1822–45 and spread

[1] Cp. Williams, W. *The Sociology of an English Village: Gosforth* (London, 1956), pp. 165–7. Williams brings out the point that the Church—in this case the Church of England—plays an important role as a binding force in the community; its influence in this respect extends beyond those who are practising members.

themselves throughout the working-class areas of the town. They contained among them persons of some education with ambitions to reach a standard of living at least equivalent to, if not better than their non-Irish labouring-class neighbours.

The original community supported a resident priest who, after 1840, was given a chapel, after making do for years with makeshift premises, and eventually built a school which met with the favour of the Commissioner of Education. A solid foundation was being laid for the Irish community to stake a claim to a position of respect and prestige in Cardiff society generally.

After 1847 this original nucleus was swamped by an influx of destitute Irish seeking refuge from the effects of the Famine. Content merely with the basic necessities of life—food and shelter— these immigrants tolerated appalling living conditions and became concentrated in one particular area of Cardiff. The fact that, by 1861, the number of such immigrants had so increased that the total Irish community formed one-third of the population of Cardiff, brought the 'Irish problem' firmly before the eyes of the local authorities and the worst of the abuses in the town—overcrowding, bad sanitation and consequent epidemics—were laid at the door of the immigrants. The evidence shows that the Irish alone were not responsible for these conditions[1]—indeed, with the tremendous increase in the town's population as the result of migration from areas in England and Wales it would be astonishing if only the Irish lived in insanitary and unhygienic housing conditions—but they formed the bulk of the population who lived in regions where such conditions existed.

The Irish community generally was relegated to a position equivalent, if not inferior to the lowest class in society. The pre-Famine immigrants, although enjoying through their earlier efforts a superior standard of living, must have shared the fate of the remainder of their fellow-countrymen who outnumbered them so heavily, and become associated in the eyes of the rest of the town with 'filth, squalor and beggarly destitution'.[2] This reaction by the non-Irish population must have been a strong reason for deciding

[1] Report of the medical officer of health, 1856, pp. 13–14.
[2] *Cardiff and Merthyr Guardian*, March, 1850.

the original settlers to throw in their lot with the recent arrivals and hence to provide them with a leadership drawn from their fellow-countrymen—a factor of great importance for the future development of the settlement.

Other factors were at work, besides the weight of outside disapproval, to bind the community together. The area inhabited by the Irish was restricted and communication between them made easy, consequently physical contact helped to make the settlement more united. Common membership of the Church and the recognition of a leader in the form of the priest also promoted the feeling of fellowship among the immigrants. This particular factor was made more important by the anti-Catholic prejudice which existed in certain quarters of the town, a prejudice which would make it appear all the more necessary for the Catholic Irish to look to one another for support.

These considerations, together with other developments which will be considered in later chapters, help to account for the fact that during the second half of the nineteenth century and the first quarter of the twentieth century the Irish settlement in Cardiff preserved characteristics which marked it off from the rest of the community and which militated against the complete assimilation of the Irish into Cardiff society.

# 6. Development of an urban community (cont'd.)

The ninety years following 1861 saw a fairly rapid development in the organisation of the Catholic community. As previously stated, it is clear that the leadership in this organisation has been taken largely by the Catholic clergy, supported by the efforts of prominent members of the lay community. Wherever there have appeared substantial numbers of Catholics living outside the original areas of settlement, a church and a school have been set up and parochial organisations formed among the local body. An examination of the development of the Irish community will largely take the form of examining the spread of Catholic parishes throughout the city and of the links which bind those parishes together. There is, in effect, the growth of a number of sub-communities inside the general Irish community, each sub-community based on a parish but with strong links binding the sub-communities into a greater whole.

In order to make the examination of the community more coherent it has been divided into several sections. For some of these sections, e.g. statistics of population and marriage tendencies among the settlers, reliable information is scarce. In the first instance, it has not been the practice of parish priests generally to keep yearly records of the total number of their parishioners—the work involved in making regular censuses is beyond their resources of time. In many parishes also, the numbers fluctuate due to the Irish people who come seeking work and, after a short stay, depart elsewhere—and, in the second case, although a record of marriages is kept in each parish the number of 'mixed' (i.e. between Catholic and non-Catholic) is not always indicated.

*Statistics of population: 1861–1951*

The following table, which has been constructed from the Census volumes, shows the number of Irish-born residents in Cardiff for the years 1861–1951.

After the peak year of 1861 the number of Irish-born persons in Cardiff has declined slowly. The flow of immigration has slowly subsided and the influx of Irish into Cardiff in the second half of

*Table 8*

Irish-born residents in Cardiff, 1861–1951[1]
(Twenty-year intervals; 1931 substituted for 1941)

| Year | Total Cardiff population | Irish-born |
|------|--------------------------|------------|
| 1861 | 32,954 | 5,000 |
| 1881 | 82,761 | 4,259 |
| 1901 | 164,333 | 3,655 |
| 1921 | 200,184 | 3,100 |
| 1931 | 223,589 | 2,332 |
| 1951 | 243,632 | 2,033 |

N.B. The figures of Irish given here are limited to those persons actually
born in Ireland. To the totals, then, must be added the second and
third generation descendants of the actual immigrants.

the nineteenth century and the first half of the twentieth century has not been as heavy as it has into many of the large English cities. The main reason for this has been that as Cardiff is not a centre of the manufacturing industry in the same way as, for example, Birmingham, the demand for labour has not been consistently high but has fluctuated according to trade on the docks and the undertaking of large building projects (e.g. the extension of the Docks and the erection of the Guest Keen Steel Works

[1] See *Irish Trade Journal and Statistical Bulletin* (Central Statistics Office, Dublin) June 1955. p. 84.

during the second half of the nineteenth century) demanding large amounts of unskilled labour.

The fact has already been noted that the majority of the immigrants during the second half of the nineteenth century belonged to the 20–25 years age group, both men and women.[1] The Cardiff community received a constant, if declining, supply of fresh blood during the ninety years following 1861 and the bulk of these immigrants settled easily into the life of the community, many of them, indeed, going to live and work with relatives or friends who had sent for them. As will be shown later, many of the young men married Irish women, who had emigrated at the same time, and founded families in Cardiff, so that the community steadily grew in size and strength.

I have pointed out already the difficulties involved in trying to make an accurate assessment of the size of the community at any one given time, but the latest figures available show that the descendants of the Irish who have remained in the religion of their predecessors and thus kept their links with the life of the group amount to approximately 30,000.[2]

### Improvement in the original area of settlement

During the second half of the nineteenth century the living conditions of the Irish who remained in the original area of settlement steadily improved. This process of improvement was assisted by several factors: the increase in the number of houses in Cardiff (which meant that there was a movement out of the settlement and a reduction in the amount of overcrowding), the strict supervision of the medical officer of health, assisted by the efforts of the Catholic clergy, which brought an improvement in standards of cleanliness and the improvement in drainage and paving of the area. These improvements had been carried out at the initiative of the local authority which was empowered by Parliament to undertake the reforms necessary to raise standards of hygiene and housing in the town. The town council was able to require both landlords

[1] Report on Emigration: *op. cit.*, p. 320 (table 29).
[2] See *Cardiff Archdiocesan Yearbook, 1956* (Cardiff), p. 79, Parish Statistics, 1954–1955.

and tenants to maintain certain standards in their houses, and improvements in paving, draining and lighting the roads and streets were carried out by the council and financed by rates levied on the residents. If people were reluctant to co-operate in this process of making their towns more fit for human beings to live in, the local council was empowered to impose penalties on them and were eventually granted powers to condemn and demolish houses which were judged unfit for human habitation.

Two other factors must also be taken into account. The peak for Irish immigration into Cardiff was reached in 1861 and after that time there was a steady decline in the numbers coming each year. There was, then, no repetition of the sudden influx which followed the Famine into an area which was not sufficiently developed to offer them adequate living room. Also, the immigrants who came in the second half of the century, did not arrive in the state of destitution characteristic of so many of their predecessors, and were better able to improve their living standards.

In Newtown and the Stanley Street area there was, then, a steady change from conditions of squalor to conditions nearer the general level existing in the working-class area of the town built in the last decades of the nineteenth century. The change did not come about rapidly. Between 1861 and 1880 improvement was slow: in 1866 conditions in the Irish quarter were still bad enough to produce a high infant mortality rate among the Irish.[1] The rents of the cottages which they occupied were still 'exorbitantly high' at this time and for several years afterwards, and this meant that a certain amount of overcrowding was inevitable.[2] The persistence of this evil and the insanitary state of the houses themselves meant that in Stanley Street, Love Lane, Mary Ann Street and the neighbouring streets living conditions remained poor. Supervision by the medical officer of health, however, had resulted in a great improvement in cleanliness and this, in turn, led to a considerable decrease in deaths from fever among the Irish.

The people themselves who lived in this region made an effort to

[1] Report of the medical officer of health, 1866, p. 19. The infant mortality rate was high in 1865 and blame is laid on the Irish and their living conditions.
[2] Report of the medical officer of health, 1869, pp. 11–12.

improve their own living conditions. An association was formed, under the leadership of the clergy, to raise standards of hygiene and to impress upon the immigrants the importance of adequate sanitary facilities.[1] The misery of those among them who were unable to find employment was given some relief through the work of an organisation in the community formed to give help in times of distress. This organisation was also led by the parish clergy.[2]

The effect of increased building was felt by the middle of the 1870's when some of the congestion in the area of the settlement was relieved. In 1878 the medical officer reported that 1,148 houses in the Cardiff urban sanitary district were occupied by Irish families.[3] Although the average number of inmates still exceeded 8 per house, the majority were living in houses which were larger than those in Stanley Street, and which were capable of housing more than one family. All these houses were strictly supervised by the medical officer. After 1880 there was a more rapid improvement than had taken place during the previous twenty years. In 1882 overcrowding had been considerably reduced from the 1869 figure; and by 1885, in spite of the fact that rents remained high, the number of overcrowded dwellings was insignificant.[4]

The improvement in the standards of cleanliness, and the resulting decline in the incidence of disease among the Irish, was maintained, and there was no repetition of the large-scale outbreaks of typhus and cholera experienced between 1847 and 1849. The officer of health, however, bemoaned the fact that certain Irish customs did not contribute to that improved standard of hygiene for which he was struggling. One factor he mentions which helped in spreading disease was the practice among the Irish of holding 'wakes' over the dead bodies of persons who had suffered from a contagious disease. At first, attempts to stop this ritual were frustrated by the tenacity with which the Irish clung to their national customs, and it was not until the officer of health asked the clergy to intervene on his behalf that the wakes were stopped. In his report the officer of health pays tribute to the work of the

[1] Cardiff Diary, 1866.
[2] *Ibid.*, March 1867.
[3] Report of the medical officer of health, 1878, p. 13.
[4] *Ibid.*, 1885, p. 59.

priests in helping to improve the living conditions of the Irish,
and says:

'. . . I received very valuable aid and co-operation from the
Catholic Clergy upon this, as upon all previous occasions,
whenever I have appealed to them.'[1]

The last occasion in the nineteenth century when the Irish were
officially connected with an outbreak of disease was in 1893. In that
year there was a typhus epidemic, which seems to have affected the
'Irish quarter' of the town more severely than other regions. This
outbreak was mentioned during a meeting of the Town Council on
19 June 1893. A letter was read to the Council from the Local
Government Board. This letter enclosed a copy of a telegram from
Fr. Butler, parish priest of St. Paul's, Tyndall Street, stating that
typhus fever existed in his parish and that no provision had been
made to have the sufferers isolated. Dr. Walford, the officer of
health, reporting to the Council on this matter, said that it was
the first outbreak of typhus fever since 1885 and it had occurred
almost exclusively in the Irish quarter of the town. Fr. Butler, he
continued, had spent a great deal of time and care on his destitute
parishioners, had visited the houses in which the first known cases
had occurred and had contracted typhus fever himself.

As a result of this comment on the part of the officer of health,
Alderman Carey had proposed and Councillor Thomas seconded
'that all the references to the Irish residents or people in the above
report of the Medical Officer of Health be eliminated'. This was
carried.[2]

I have quoted the report concerning the wakes and the incident
of 1893 because they are significant not only for the way in which
they indicate improvement in the conditions of the Irish, but also
for points developed in later sections. Both these matters show the
important role played by the priest in the life of the Irish, outside
of the exercise of his purely spiritual functions.

The latter incident demonstrates the fact that individual Irish-

---

[1] *Ibid.*, 1876, p. 25.
[2] Cardiff Town Council Minutes. 19 June 1893. (*Cardiff Records.* Vol. 5,
p. 178.)

men were able to muster sufficient support on the Town Council to suppress in official reports references to the Irish which could be interpreted as critical of their mode of life.

During these years when living conditions improved, the community itself took shape.

As the population grew, the church which had been built in 1841 proved to be inadequate; in order to meet the requirements of the Irish who had moved into the Tyndall Street area, a chapel was opened there in 1873. This, in turn, proved to be too small and in 1893 the Church of St. Paul's was opened and the area was made into a separate parish. By this time the original St. David's Church had been replaced by a larger building in Charles Street, and this latter church, which was to become St. David's Cathedral, was consecrated in 1887.

The interval between the building of these churches—symbols of the increasing substance of the community—saw also a considerable increase in the educational facilities at the disposal of the Irish. The work of improving the educational standards of the community had been entrusted almost entirely to one man—Fr. Signini, a member of the Institute of Charity, and it was through his efforts that the foundations of the school system were laid throughout the parishes of Cardiff. In 1865 there were two schools in David Street, catering for the children of the settlers.[1] They were staffed largely by the members of religious orders, the girl's school being run by the Sisters of Providence and the boy's school by the Brothers of the Institute of Charity.

The response by parents to the establishment of these schools was not, at first, enthusiastic. On the first day that they opened there was a total attendance of approximately 380 children, made up of 135 boys, 130 girls and 120 infants. The total population of the community was more than 10,000 and so the percentage of children sent to school was likely to have been small. This is not surprising, for the factors outlined in Section 2 influencing parents' willingness or ability to send their children to school still held sway. Persistent efforts on the part of the clergy to persuade the immigrants of the necessity of education for their children began to bear

[1] Cardiff Diary of the Fathers of Charity, October 1885.

fruit, and by 1865 the school population had increased to almost one thousand.[1]

This encouraged Fr. Signini to embark on a more ambitious project than merely providing elementary education for the Irish. In 1867 another school was opened in David Street to cater for those children who wished to remain at school beyond the elementary stage. This institution, called variously a 'middle' school and a 'grammar' school, was put under the direction of a Brother of the Institute of Charity, Brother Bird, and given the title 'St. Joseph's Grammar School'. The attendance at the first day of opening amounted to 11 boys and 'an increase in the number of girls'. No indication exists of the actual number of girls there were so that it is impossible to arrive at a final total figure. As Brother Bird, however, is the only teacher mentioned, it is reasonable to assume that the total number of pupils would not have exceeded 70 at the most. The fact that only eleven boys remained at school beyond the elementary stage indicates that at this time only a small percentage of Irish parents were prepared to sacrifice the earning power of their children in order to give them further education. As the schools of the community developed in order to keep pace with changes in the state system of education, St. Joseph's merged its identity with the other schools in David Street, and eventually became the senior section of the 'all-age' school that existed there prior to the 1944 Education Act.

Finance for these schools was gained almost entirely from voluntary contribution from members of the community itself and from persons outside it.[2] The immigrants themselves could not have borne the burden alone and, in this respect, the widespread contacts of the clergy were useful. Money for Fr. Signini's work came from Europe, particularly Italy where, it is noted in the Diary, Cavour's brother made a donation to assist the school building fund. In Cardiff itself the priest enlisted the aid of a wide variety of subscribers—he even included the ships which came into the docks on his itinerary when searching for money—and tradition has it that one of his most substantial benefactors was the Superintendent of the Cardiff Police. This method of raising money,

[1] *Ibid.*, 4 August 1865.                              [2] *Ibid.*, April 1867.

entailing, as it did, self-sacrifice on the part of the community, serves to emphasise the importance they placed on the establishment of their own schools, and the significance they attached to retaining complete control over the education of their children. This characteristic is still much in evidence today and the struggle to maintain a system of education independent of the state is an important element in keeping alive the feeling of kinship among the Irish Catholic communities to be found in most cities.

There were other elements for the development of an educational system important in shaping the Irish Cardiff community, e.g. social and political organisations, but, as these affected the whole of the Cardiff Irish community and not just one particular section of it I have dealt with them under separate headings.

At the end of the nineteenth century, conditions in the original area of settlement had reached the stage where the Irish were living in houses and under conditions which were similar to those in any other working-class area of the town. Improvements in living conditions had been accompanied by a rise in educational facilities and a general movement out of the conditions of apathy and squalor which had prevailed in the years of the mid-century. Since 1900 there has been a further change in the character of this region. With the expansion of Cardiff the population has moved out of the Stanley Street-Newtown area into the new working-class suburbs and council estates: the parish of St. David's now numbers just over 2,000 as opposed to 10,000 in 1861 and the parish of St. Paul's which, when established, attended to the needs of approximately 2,000 Irish, now has a population of only 690.[1]

The physical appearance of the region is also changing rapidly as the old houses are demolished. Stanley Street still bears its nameplate but there are no longer any houses in it, and Mary Ann Street now harbours warehouses and offices. Similar changes are taking place in Newtown and the possibility is that, in the future, all traces of the Irish settlement there will have disappeared, and the descendants of the original settlers will have established themselves in other working-class areas of the city.

[1] *Cardiff Archdiocesan Yearbook*, 1956 (*op. cit.*) p. 79.

*Movement into other areas: spread of the Catholic community*

During the second half of the nineteenth century the increased
commercial importance of Cardiff brought about a rapid expansion
in the size of the town. New areas, particularly around the docks
and other centres of industry were developed as suburbs to house
the working class while, at the same time, more substantial dwellings began to be erected close to the town centre to be occupied by
the prosperous merchants and traders.

As the town itself grew, so sections of the Irish community
moved out of the area of settlement and into the new working-class
regions that were being built. The number of those who moved
from Newtown and Stanley Street into Roath, Canton, Grangetown and, later, Splott, were added to by the immigrants who came
from Ireland during the second half of the century. These newcomers sought accommodation in the areas close to their place of
work and many of them settled with relatives or friends who had
come to Cardiff earlier. As a result, the later years of the nineteenth
century and the first quarter of the twentieth century see the
development of a number of Irish sub-communities in the town
which are linked together by organisations common to them all.
During the last twenty years numbers of the descendants of the
Irish have moved into the residential suburbs of the city and some
attempt must be made to trace this movement also.

In order to avoid the confusion which could result from an
examination of movement with other areas according to strict
chronological order, I have taken each area of the settlement individually and dealt with its growth from 1861–1951. A general view
of the whole movement of the Irish population between these dates,
however, will help to set the growth of each sub-community in
perspective.

In Chapter 2 the initial founding of the settlement around
Stanley Street and the movement to Newtown has been described.
By 1861 further developments had taken place, for in that year
there was a substantial number of Irish living in Roath. By the
middle of the 1860's Irish families were occupying houses in
Grangetown and Canton, two districts which developed practically
simultaneously. Twenty years later there had been a tremendous

increase in the size of the Roath district and a thriving Irish community was established; Grangetown and Canton had also grown in size and at this time the groups in both places were over 1,000 strong. The concentration of a number of industries near the Roath Dock had led to the building of houses near them and, as a result, the district of Splott had come into existence by 1886.

At the end of the century Roath, Canton, Grangetown and Splott had been completed, except for minor additions made during the last thirty years. In each of these districts there was a group of Irish families concentrating their activities around church and school, two institutions which were the symbols of their existence as communities.

The twentieth century sees the development of areas on the outskirts of the city—residential suburbs and council estates. At the end of the first decade of this century, Penylan had come into existence and the residential area around Victoria Park, at the other side of the town, was in the process of development. During the course of the next twenty years extensive building was carried out on the northern, eastern and western outskirts of Cardiff so that by 1930, Birchgrove, Cyncoed, Rumney, Fairwater and Heath had found their place on the map, Llandaff and Whitchurch had increased in size and a start had been made on the council estate at Ely. In each of these areas members of the Cardiff Irish community were to be found though, as might be expected, prior to 1951, there were heavier concentrations of them in the working-class areas of Roath, Canton, Grangetown and Splott and in the council estates than there were in suburbs like Whitchurch and Cyncoed.

The largest of the Irish communities which developed outside the original area of settlement was that concentrated in the Roath area around St. Peter's Church. The district itself developed very rapidly during the second half of the century due, probably, to two reasons—it lay within easy reach of the docks and, as it lay largely on the north side of Queen Street, it had attractions purely as a residential area. As a result, Roath contains buildings of varying quality, from small cottage-type properties which were inhabited mainly by the working class, to large imposing houses which were occupied by traders and merchants.

The Irish population of Roath also increased fairly rapidly during this period. In 1861 there were approximately one thousand parishioners of St. Peter's; this figure had increased to 1,800 by 1877 and had reached 3,500 by 1886.[1] The organisation of these people into a community followed a pattern which was to be repeated in every other area of Cardiff. The first essential institution, the Church, was established in 1861 and the organisation spread outwards from there. In 1868 a school was opened on a site near the church. It was held in a building which had once been a Wesleyan Chapel and the staff consisted of one schoolmaster—Timothy O'Brien—who previously had run his own private school in a street near the church.[2] It was felt, however, that it would be more satisfactory to transfer Mr. O'Brien to premises which were larger and which came under the direct control of the clergy rather than to utilise his own establishment as a school for the Irish children.[3]

No details are available of the number of children who attended at the opening of the school but an account is given of the financial arrangements involved. This shows that the expenses for running the school came to £12 per annum, which figure included the rent for the building.[4] There is no mention of any salary for the master-in-charge—who was not a qualified teacher—but he did receive his room rent-free. Presumably he gained his livelihood from the contributions of his pupils.

A site was quickly obtained for the building of a new school and in 1872 the school was opened, catering for both boys and girls.[5] It was divided in the following year into separate boys' and girls' schools and two new teachers were appointed—a man to take charge of the boys' section and a woman to look after the girls and infants. The schools were extended in 1902. In 1878 a more ambitious project was begun and a building was purchased to be used as a 'high class' girls' school and the Rosminian nuns were installed there.[6]

[1] Cardiff Diary of the Fathers of Charity: Census, 1886.
[2] *Ibid.*, 14 January 1868.
[3] *Ibid.*
[4] *Ibid.*
[5] *Ibid.*, 5 August 1872.                    [6] *Ibid.*, 4 April 1878.

Thus, by the end of the century, the community in Roath had a school available for their children which provided an elementary education on a par with the 'board' schools in the town. For those who could afford it, there was a school for girls which provided education up to the standard required for entry to the professions. In these developments the initiative, as in Newtown, had been taken by the clergy and it was through their efforts that the community had its own educational system. The burden of financing such a system fell largely upon the community itself. Money was gained through contributions from each household, through organised campaigns to raise finance and, in some cases, through appeals to Catholics in other parts of Britain and in Ireland.

The appointment of staff to the schools was the duty of the priest in charge. It is noticeable that whereas lay folk from within the Irish community were, in 1873, able to undertake teaching at an elementary stage (following Mr. O'Brien at St. Peter's were Mr. Timothy Donovan and Miss C. Higgins), the teaching at the high school had to be entrusted to the care of a religious order which sent members to Cardiff from other parts of the country. A strong argument in favour of this was that the religious would not require payment for their work and would, in consequence, be less of a strain on the financial resources of the community. The call upon the religious also demonstrates the fact that the community itself could not provide teachers of a sufficient level of attainment to cope with the work involved.

Only a very rough assessment can be given of the numbers of the Irish community in Canton during the second half of the nineteenth century. There were sufficient there to justify the establishment of a school, with one teacher, before 1865, but the total would not have reached 1,000 before this date.[1] In 1877 the total had reached 1,100[2] and, as the area developed in size during the last years of the nineteenth century so the Irish community increased also until in 1954 it numbered approximately 4,000.[3]

The living conditions of Newtown, described in Section 2, did

---

[1] *Ibid.*, March 1865.
[2] Log book of the Church of St Mary of the Angels, Canton, Cardiff.
[3] *Cardiff Archdiocesan Year Book*, 1956, p. 79.

not apply to Canton. The immigrants there occupied terraced houses which were of superior construction and size to those in the centre of the town and which, consequently, encouraged higher living standards.

The first attempt to organise the community was made before 1865 when a small school was set up. In 1869 the number of immigrants had increased sufficiently to demand the services of a priest and so, in that year, the school-room was used as a chapel and Mass was said there.[1] Some years later, when accommodation in the school-room became inadequate, a temporary structure was put up to serve as a church and this remained the centre of the community until the present Church of St. Mary of the Angels was opened in 1907.

Once a centre of worship had been secured, attention was turned to the problem of education. In 1865 the school was which already in existence was placed on a more regular footing. The person who had been running it was replaced by a qualified teacher—a woman —and, on the opening day, 80 children between 4–12 years were enrolled. The accommodation soon proved inadequate for the needs of the community and in 1868 a plot was bought in Wyndham Crescent for £250 on which to build a new school. School attendance increased steadily until, in 1877, the number on the school roll had reached 106. The school was enlarged to meet this growing demand until, by 1930, there were three schools on the Wyndham Crescent site—an infant school, a junior school and a secondary school. The latter school catered exclusively for pupils in the 11–14 age group and, as a result, was a departure from the practice common in state as well as Catholic schools of building 'all age' schools catering for the 7–14 age group. It may be claimed, indeed, that the 'senior' school in St. Mary's was a forerunner of the present secondary modern school, anticipating the Education Act of 1944 by some twenty years. The infant and junior schools were placed under the direction of a religious order (the Ursuline Sisters at first, followed by the Sisters of St. John of God) assisted by some lay teachers, and the secondary school was staffed by lay teachers under the direction of a lay headmaster.

[1] Cardiff Diary of the Fathers of Charity, 22 August 1869.

The methods of financing the education system followed the pattern already described for Newtown and Roath. In 1865 the Poor Law Authority provided 2½d per head per week for boys and girls attending the school and 1½d per head for infants of parents who were receiving outdoor relief. This, combined with the voluntary contributions, enabled the school to be run reasonably smoothly; but when more ambitious schemes were attempted, the community suffered a setback. In 1868 work had to be stopped on the new school because of lack of funds. £350 had already been spent by that date out of the private sources of the Institute of Charity and £220 more was to be used out of Fr. Signini's 'inheritance'.[1] This still left £400 needed before the work could be completed. In July 1869 Fr. Signini held a meeting in the schoolroom in Canton and arrangements were made for a weekly collection of 1d or ½d to be made from each household in order to meet the cost of the new school.[2] Such measures had the same success in Canton as they did in Roath and Newtown for the schools managed to flourish and expand throughout the nineteenth century.[3]

The development of the Grangetown branch of the Irish community proceeded along lines very similar to those of Canton. The population in Grangetown was sufficient to warrant the establishment of a school there before 1865 and by 1877 the immigrants totalled 500 approximately.[4] By 1954 this number had grown to 3,000.[5]

As in Canton, the school-room was used as a centre for saying Mass in 1869 and, when the numbers and financial strength of the settlers had grown, a church was opened in 1883. This building eventually proved to be inadequate in size and a new and much bigger church was built in 1930.

In 1873 a mixed school was opened in Thomas Street and by 1877 there were 301 children on its roll, with an average attendance

---

[1] *Ibid.*, 14 December 1868.     [2] *Ibid.*, 11 July 1869.

[3] Some relief was received in 1877 in the form of a government grant of £62 14s 9d; to be shared between the schools in Canton and Grangetown.

See Log book of St. Mary of the Angels, Canton, and Cardiff Diary of the Fathers of Charity, November 1877.

[4] Cardiff Diary of the Fathers of Charity, November 1877.

[5] *Cardiff Archdiocesan Year Book*, 1956, p. 79.

of 108. As the numbers of children increased the church itself had to be used as an infant school during the week until, in 1897, a school was built to accommodate these younger children. In 1901 the mixed schools themselves were extended by the addition of two classrooms estimated to hold 120 children. These original buildings have remained, with the addition of two classrooms, to the present day. The finance for these buildings was raised once more by voluntary contributions.

I have examined the development of institutions in the areas of Newtown, Roath, Canton and Grangetown in some detail in order to show that the organisation of these scattered groups of Catholics throughout the town followed a clear pattern. The basic needs of the group—church and school—were provided immediately there were sufficient numbers to warrant the expense, and it was upon these that the community life of each area was based. It is, I think, important to realise this similarity in development because it played a large part in linking up the areas and in uniting Catholics throughout Cardiff as a whole. An immigrant living in Grangetown, although separated by some distance from one living in Roath, nevertheless lived in an exactly similar community life and had bonds of kinship with him. Similarly, the movement of a Catholic family from one part of the town to another did not mean a break with the community life to which its members were accustomed; it merely entailed their settling into the same life with the old familiar institutions in another region of the town.

Because of the similarity in development, the growth of Irish sub-communities in other parts of Cardiff than those examined need not be gone into in detail. In the closing years of the nineteenth century the Splott area was provided with a temporary church (1897) and a new church was opened in 1911. Schools were built in the succeeding years. In 1913 a temporary church was erected at Heath, a school was opened in 1927 and a new church built in 1936. The Whitchurch district was provided with a church in 1927—no school here because of insufficient demand—and two churches were erected in Ely, the first in 1927 and the second in 1932. The growth of the community in Ely led to the building of schools in the centre of the council estate there. Finally, the areas of Rumney (1931) and Leckwith (1937) were provided with churches; in the case of the former area, the population has expanded to such an extent due to the development of a large council estate close at hand, that schools—infant and junior— were opened there in 1958.

By 1954 there were thirteen churches in Cardiff and schools were attached to eight of these. These institutions served a total population of approximately 30,000.[1] Two schools need particular mention. The 'high-class' girls' school which was established in Roath in 1878 has developed into the Heathfield House High School, the Catholic grammar school to which the daughters of the Cardiff community go from the junior schools. In 1922, a Catholic grammar school for boys—St. Illtyd's College—was opened in Splott and boys from all the city parishes go there from the parish schools. The effect of these schools in preparing the descendants of the Irish settlers for integration into Cardiff society will be discussed in a later section but it must be mentioned here that the fact that these schools draw their pupils from all sections of the town seems to have given them, through their close daily contact with children from other parishes, an added sense of the unity of the community throughout Cardiff. This factor is now at work in other sections of the educational system owing to the establishment in 1956 and 1957 of two large secondary modern schools which draw their pupils also from all parts of the city. The result is that, whereas in the past only a relatively small proportion of children left their parish schools to go to the two central establishments, leaving behind a substantial number who had begun and ended their school life in the same building and in the same district, now a steadily increasing number is leaving the parishes to complete their education. It may be that these developments will have the effect of weakening loyalties to one particular parish.[2]

## Social activities

The development of each branch of the Catholic community was not restricted to the building of churches and the establishment of

---

[1] *Ibid.*, p. 79.
[2] See the studies by Dr Joan Brothers listed in the Bibliography, in particular her book *Church and School* (University of Liverpool, 1964).

schools. Some account has already been given of attempts to organise leisure activities among the people before 1861, and these efforts were continued on a larger scale during the second half of the nineteenth century. By 'social activities' is meant not only activities of a recreational nature but also activities undertaken in common and aimed at improving the general level of life of the immigrants. The lead in most of these activities was taken by the clergy because they were looked upon by Catholics as their natural leaders.

In order to strengthen the sense of community among their flock, and in order to ensure that as full and as active a part as possible was played in the life of the Church, great emphasis was placed on parochial organisations. Once the essential building programme of church and school was completed, attention was focused on providing a suitable meeting place for the people of the parish. In many cases, where funds were not sufficient to meet the cost of building a hall, the school-room, and even the church itself, was used for this purpose. Thus, in each district where groups of Irish have settled, organisations have been set up with their headquarters on the church premises; and in this way the church has become the focal point of an important sector of the lives of the people. (I exclude from these comments those organisations of a specifically political nature which grew up among the Cardiff Irish and which will be dealt with under a separate heading.)

The Diary of the Fathers of Charity throws considerable light on the early attempts in the 1860's to organise some social life among the Irish. The priests of St. Peter's and St. David's organised tea-parties for the children in the school-room, took them on outings (one trip to Batty's Menagerie receiving special note) and even started a 'little boys' band'. The adults were not forgotten either; plays and farces were provided as entertainment, again in the school-room, and a Hibernian band, possibly a descendant of Brother Colton's fife and drum band, mentioned in Chapter 2, flourished at this time. This sort of light-hearted activity, however, was merely a small part of a much larger sphere of activity, demanded by the social conditions of the time.

The living conditions of the Irish in the middle of the century ensured that organised activity among them should be aimed at improving their standard of living and eliminating some of the distress under which a section of them suffered. Drunkenness remained a great problem during the third quarter of the nineteenth century and the Rev. Fr. Richardson continued his campaign against this particular evil. In 1862, two organisations existed to combat the effect of drink—the Teetotallers and the Temperance Society.[1] The Temperance Society came directly under Fr. Richardson's control, but the Teetotallers (so-called) proved to be something of a nuisance. They were, apparently, inclined to be sensitive about the appointment of their president and proved rather a thorn in the flesh of the clergy.[2] In spite of such difficulties, however, the campaign—re-styled the 'Holy War Crusade'—prospered. Throughout the 1860's public meetings were held in the schools and in the Temperance Hall, meetings at which the corrupting influence of alcohol was brought sharply home to the community. By 1868, 400 had joined the Temperance Society: no more is heard of the Teetotallers.[3]

An attempt was also made to bring home the advantages of thrift and prudence to the community, and in 1868 a Penny Bank was established by the Rector of St. Peter's.[4] The operating of this sort of scheme, taken in conjunction with the work of the association aimed at improving sanitary conditions, and the relief organisation which had been set up—both of which have been mentioned earlier —must have helped the Irish to improve their living conditions and to have increased their tendency towards reliance for help upon the community itself and not upon outside bodies. In 1889 and 1890 the social work took an important step forward with the foundation, on those two dates, of branches of the St. Vincent de Paul Society in St. David's and St. Peter's. The aim of this society is to assist members of the community in times of distress due to illness or unemployment and particular attention is paid to families left fatherless. The society draws its membership from the men of the community and as the population has grown, branches have been established in every part of Cardiff.

---

[1] See the Cardiff Diary of the Fathers of Charity for 1862.
[2] *Ibid.*          [3] *Ibid.*, March 1868.          [4] *Ibid.*, January 1868.

The activities of the Society of St. Vincent de Paul (S.V.P.) are directed by a group of men in each parish and these officers are responsible to an area council covering a group of parishes. A central council controls the work in a particular area, e.g. in South Wales there is one Central Council based on Cardiff and containing representatives of Swansea, Aberavon and Newport. The clergy is represented on this Council by a chaplain.

The members of the S.V.P. are bound by strict rules of secrecy so that no details are available of their work. Obviously the existence of such a highly organised voluntary body must have made a valuable contribution to the work of removing the problem of destitution among the Irish. The help of such a body would also be more acceptable to the members of the community who needed assistance than that of charitable organisations outside the community—the helpers were of their own kind, understood their problems and were able to gain their confidence.

During the first half of this century, a multiplicity of organisations under the direction of the clergy has grown up in Cardiff.[1] Most of these organisations have branches in each parish which are linked through a central body, and they all serve to bring together the members of the community during their leisure hours. The primary purpose of these societies is to combine business with pleasure, i.e. they cater for recreational as well as more serious activities, and an attempt is made to ensure that every Catholic adult belongs to one or more of them. In this way, not only is the community spirit kept alive but also the group has a means, when occasion demands it, of taking organised action, e.g. combined activities to raise funds for school building or the preservation of the 'Catholic case' on political issues.

---

[1] These organisations include: Cardiff Archdiocesan Child Rescue and Mora Welfare Society; Cardiff and District Catholic Teacher's Association; Cardiff Catholic Social Guild; Catholic Needlework Guild; Catholic Scout Guild; Catholic Truth Society; Catholic Women's League; Catholic Young Men's Society; Catholic Nurses Guild; Civil Service Catholic Guild; Guild of St. Luke, Cosmos and Damian (for Catholic doctors); Knights of St. Columba; the Catenian Association; Legion of Mary; Cardiff Catholic Institute for Seamen; and the Union of Catholic Mothers.

There is also the Catholic Society for University Students in Cardiff and the Cardiff Newman Circle which caters for University graduates.

Unlike the organisations described above, The Ancient Order of Hibernians which was in existence in the earliest years of the community's life, has been completely under the control of laymen. The origin of the 'Hibernians' has already been described in a previous chapter. The original members of the order—the more prosperous of the early immigrants—continued their activities during the second half of the century and as their members grew due to the increasing prosperity of the community, so the organisation itself expanded. Its aims were to provide a social organisation, and to encourage thrift among the settlers by providing them with savings and a rudimentary insurance scheme. By 1874 sufficient progress had been made along these lines for the establishment of the Hibernian Benefit Building Society.

The work of this society had two main aspects. The 'benefit' section provided a scheme whereby in return for small weekly contributions from its members payment was made during times of sickness or unemployment. The 'building' section existed to encourage home ownership among the members of the community through the advance of loans for house purchase. Unfortunately no records are available of the scope of these activities before 1896, which is the date of the oldest extant balance sheet of the Building Society. At this date the building and benefit sections, though still occupying the same offices and remaining under the control of the Order, had been divided into two self-contained organisations. The

*Table 9:* Hibernian Building Society, 1896–1957.[1]

| Year | Amount on loan for house purchase |
|------|-----------------------------------|
| 1896 | £4,000 |
| 1910 | £9,000 |
| 1920 | £24,751 |
| 1930 | £25,182 |
| 1940 | £44,529 |
| 1950 | £94,284 |
| 1957 | £408,000 |

[1] The figures in this table have been taken from the balance sheets of the Hibernian Building Society for the years mentioned.

Hibernian Benefit Society remained in existence until the National
Insurance Act made its work no longer necessary. but the Hibernian
Building Society has gone from strength to strength during the
first half of this century. The table on page 117 shows how it has
expanded.

Since it was not the practice of the Society, prior to 1951, to
advertise for business, or generally attempt to make its name known
outside the Irish community in Cardiff, it is fairly safe to assume
that the bulk of its lending was restricted to members of the community. The fall in the value of the pound sterling during the
period 1896–1957 must obviously be taken into account when the
increase in the amount of money on loan for house purchase is
considered. Even so, the table throws an interesting side-light on
the growth of home-ownership among the Irish and is some
indication of their growing prosperity.

The two branches of the Hibernians—benefit and building—
were controlled throughout the life of the organisation down to
1951 by a group of men drawn from within the community. The
occupation of these men varied, but most of them were skilled
workers or small tradesmen who devoted their spare time to the
affairs of the two societies. The work of the two societies gives a
remarkable example of self-help and initiative on the part of men
who were, for the most part, unversed in the skills of even relatively high finance, yet who were prepared to take the risk of
lending money to their fellow Irish to provide them with homes.
The technical difficulties involved in house purchase presented
some problems at first. Fortunately the Hibernian directors were
able to obtain the services of a solicitor who was also a prominent
member of the community, and thus were saved from becoming
involved in legal tangles, but the other aspects of house buying—
surveying and valuing—they performed themselves. The suitability
of candidates for loans was tested by the standing of their families
in the community or by a recommendation from one of the clergy.

The Building Society was run largely along these lines until
1951. In that year a full-time secretary was appointed, and the
affairs of the Society were established on a basis nearer to that of
its fellow Building Societies. The board of directors still draws its

membership from the local Irish community—one of the directors has been associated with the Hibernians for over 40 years—but the ancestry of these men is now the only link with the Hibernian Society of the past.

The importance of the Hibernians was not restricted to the activities described above. The Order acted, also, as a social body which united, in its functions, all the more prosperous members of the community. The Hibernian's celebrations on St. Patrick's Day were the social events of the year and were much commented upon by the local press. The Order did not play such a prominent part in the processions on St. Patrick's Day in the twentieth century, as they had throughout the nineteenth century—by the turn of the century the organisation of these demonstrations had been taken over almost entirely by the clergy, and the accent was placed mainly on the religious significance of the feast day—but the custom of holding a dinner was followed until the 1930's. All these activities have now lapsed, however, and the Ancient Order of Hibernians in Cardiff is defunct. The Building Society has no connection with the Order and the memory of the latter's activities is preserved only by the name of what was one of its most fruitful projects.

## Class divisions within the community

It has been noted previously that there was an internal division within the community at the start of the settlement and that most of the members of the more substantial 'class' came before the influx which followed the Famine. This division was perpetuated through the years of distress in the middle of the nineteenth century and since 1860 there has been a steady growth in the small number of Irish who have moved from the working-class into the lower middle group. Those who have made this progress fall fairly evenly into two sections—those who have achieved prosperity by opening small family businesses and those who, drawing upon their rural upbringing, have combined a full-time job in industry with the running of a small-holding. Many of the descendants of the immigrants, who now occupy positions in the professions or who have achieved some standing in the business world, can trace the start of their prosperity to the opening of the family shop or the leasing of the family acre. A very small number who came over before 1861 were able to open small schools or take jobs as teachers in the parish schools and joined the ranks of the lower-middle class. There have also been a number of Irish doctors who have come to the town at various times at the end of the nineteenth and beginning of the twentieth century. They set up practice in the working-class areas where there were large groups of Irish and occupied positions of esteem and influence in the Irish community.

During the second half of the century, one or two Irish families of substantial means settled in Cardiff but their numbers were so small as to be insignificant and they have not settled in Cardiff permanently or become part of the Irish community.

By 1860 there were three Irish tradesmen whose names appeared in the Cardiff Directory—a druggist, a tobacconist and the proprietor of a potato store.[1] During the following decades an increasing number of Irish names appear among the list of tradesmen in the town. They include among them grocers, tobacconists, chemists, drapers and a number of publicans. The growing prosperity of Cardiff brought increased trade to these people and as their wealth grew so their choice of an area in which to live became wider so that Irish families appear in the 'superior' sections of Roath, Canton and Grangetown by the end of the century.

The children of these families, still relatively small in number at the start of the twentieth century, were able to profit by their parents' increased means and some of them began to enter the professions, particularly school-teaching. This movement was, however, practically restricted to the daughters of the family because of the lack of educational facilities beyond the elementary stage for boys in the town.[2] As the residential suburbs of Cardiff

[1] See *Cardiff Directory*, 1855.
[2] As a result of this factor, schoolteaching seems to have been regarded by the community as largely the province of women. It was common for the junior or elementary section of the parish schools to be staffed entirely by women, and this situation is only slowly drawing to an end. There is, in fact, in Cardiff one Catholic junior school still staffed entirely by women, and one other such school had men appointed to the staff for the first time in 1957. In junior schools run entirely by the local education authority the ratio of staff is maintained as far as possible at an equal division between men and women.

began to develop in the first quarter of this century, there was some movement of these Irish into areas like Penylan, Heath and Whitchurch. This movement has continued during the last thirty years so that groups of the descendants of the original settlers in Cardiff are to be found in every part of the city.

Movement away from working-class status and area did not mean that links with the community were broken. If anything such links were strengthened by the process as the people concerned began to play an increasingly important part in the community life. The daughters of the immigrants who had made sufficient money to send them to a training college after their period at Heathfield House, returned to teach in the town, often in the parish schools where they had received their early education, and this removed some of the burden of work from the religious orders. The local tradesman was called upon to supply the catering needs for the many social activities which took place in the parishes, particularly at Christmas time, and was expected to provide the prizes for the parish prize-draw in aid of the church or school building fund. The Irish doctor was assured of a large practice, if he set himself up in the right area, composed of patients who would accept his word as law and afford him something of the esteem that was given to the priest.

There grew up, in each area of the community, a small nucleus composed of these lower-middle class Irish. This nucleus provided the clergy with persons fitted to take the leading roles in the many associations and organisations that had been formed. Their names were known and respected amongst the Irish themselves and their presence on the parish committees meant that the burden of work involved in raising money for the maintenance and building of churches and schools, running youth clubs and organisations like scout and guide troops, organising delegations to interview parliamentary candidates at election times and even giving religious instructions to the children of the community, could be lifted from the clergy and taken over by the laymen and women. In all these activities the priest held a watching brief but the day-to-day organisation of them passed out of his hands.

In this way the slow division of the community into two main classes, far from destroying the unity of the group, helped to maintain it and strengthen it. The Irish saw their organisations directed by people who had risen from among them and responded to the lead accordingly; the man who had 'made good' found an opportunity to fulfil his desires for the responsibility of leadership in the life of his own community.

## Inter-marriage tendencies

Any examination of this aspect of the life of the community is hampered by several factors. The marriage registers of the churches in Cardiff would show only those members who were married inside the Church and, therefore, would only cover a proportion of the total. It is impossible to arrive at any precise estimate of the number of Irish Catholics who married outside the Church and, as a result, broke away from the community. Furthermore, until the last twenty years, it was not always indicated in the marriage registers when a marriage was 'mixed', i.e. between a Catholic and a non-Catholic, and it is only through adding the number of non-Irish names which appear before this time that a rough estimate can be made of the total. It is clear, then, that all that can be hoped for on the basis of such information as is available on this point, is an approximation of the trends towards marrying outside the community during the years of its establishment and development. For this purpose I have analysed the registers of St. Mary's Church, Canton: this particular church was chosen because it ministers to a typical cross-section of the Irish community and, as has been shown in Chapter 2, the Canton branch of the Cardiff community has developed along the same lines as those of all other sections in the city. Marriage tendencies in this area would reflect general tendencies throughout the community—a fact which is supported by the recent publication of figures showing the total number of mixed marriages in the city in 1955.[1]

It has already been noted in Chapter 2 that the earliest Irish immigrants tended to marry within the community. As the community developed this tendency remained stable, at least until the third quarter of the nineteenth century. The names in the registers

[1] *Cardiff Archdiocesan Year Book*, 1956, p. 79.

of St. Mary's covering the years between 1875–96 show an increase in the number of English and Welsh names appearing. In 1910 when the first definite record of mixed marriages appears these amounted to 6 out of a total of 18. In 1922 the total number of mixed marriages had reached 25 out of a total of 43 and in 1930 the figures were 27 out of 41. The apparently haphazard selection of dates is caused by the fact that not all of the officiating clergy took the trouble to note the fact that a marriage was mixed. Thus the register for 1920 shows 2 mixed marriages out of a total of 50 and for 1921, 1 out of 38; figures very difficult to accept at their face value when set alongside those already quoted.

The registers show, then, that although by the end of the nineteenth century the bulk of the marriages were still within the community, there was a growing tendency for the Irish to seek their partners from among people outside. This tendency has increased during the twentieth century and, by 1910, one-third of the marriages performed were between Irish and non-Irish and by 1920 the proportion had reached approximately 55 per cent. The percentage rose in 1930 to approximately 66 but the latest figures published seem to show that the average number since that date has been between 50–60 per cent.[1]

The fact that roughly half of the members of the community, who marry in church, marry outside their circle does not necessarily mean that their links with the community are immediately broken. For the children of such marriages, however, their sphere of activities must inevitably extend beyond the bounds of the group. Although they are brought up as Catholics and are therefore reared within the same educational framework as children of entirely Catholic marriages, their ties of family and kinship extend into non-Catholic spheres and their contacts are much wider. In some cases this can lead to a clash of loyalties which may result in a total lapsing from membership of the Church and the community; in others, the non-Catholic partner in the marriage may be converted to Catholicism and become absorbed into the community. Where neither of these eventualities occur, the children become 'middle-men', belonging fully neither to the community nor to the society

[1] *Ibid.*

outside it. If they, in turn, are partners in 'mixed' marriages then it seems likely that their movement away from the community will be stimulated; however, the difficulties outlined at the start of this section preclude any accurate estimate of the rate at which the integration of the Irish community with the rest of Cardiff society is proceeding through intermarriage. All that can safely be said is that the percentage of mixed marriages, supplemented by the unknown number of Irish who marry outside the Church, is bringing about a blending of the Irish and their neighbours in Cardiff.

*Relationship between Catholics and their social environment in Cardiff*

The development of the relationship of the members of the Catholic community in Cardiff to their fellow-townspeople outside the community seems to be following a pattern which has something in common with the process of assimilation experienced by other minority groups placed in similar situations.[1] The development of the community, in two respects, falls into two main phases: a period of isolation, when contact with the group outside was slight and restricted to relatively few members of the community, and a period when this isolation is being broken down and the community shows signs of assimilation with the outside. The outbreak of the Second World War contributed a great deal to the ending of the period of isolation; there were, during the ten years before 1939, signs that the Irish were beginning to filter into the general social framework of Cardiff, but the war accelerated the process of breaking down the barriers, and the years immediately following 1945 have seen further developments in this direction.

The causes of the isolation of the Irish community during the nineteenth century and the first decades of the twentieth century are to be found in influences operating inside and outside the community itself. The opposition to the Irish from outside the community was based largely on three grounds—religious, social and national. These three were linked, often inextricably, to produce a feeling of hostility towards the immigrants, but they have been divided in order to show more clearly the elements of anti-Irish feeling.

Of these three factors, religion was the first and most important.

[1] See Section 7.

As the evidence given below will show, it is plain right from the start of the Irish immigration that sections of the Cardiff residents looked with great apprehension on the probability of a restoration of Catholicism in the town and were prepared to exert as much pressure as possible to prevent it. In 1826 a poster appeared in the town exhorting all the protestant burgesses to defend themselves against the encroachment of popery and to refuse their vote to any member of Parliament who sought to give increased rights or freedom to Catholics.[1] This condemnation of Catholicism was in general terms and did not apply specifically to Cardiff, but it shows the prevailing feeling among at least a section of the more substantial class in the region.

There were, also, a number of outspoken attacks on Catholicism in the local newspaper between 1842 and 1861 and there is no doubt that they represented the views of a number of people of influence in the town at the time.[2] This is demonstrated by the difficulties encountered, by the first immigrants in securing a site for a church. Before the building of St. David's a site had been found in another position but due to what was called 'the inveterate prejudice and intense bigotry of the inhabitants and landed proprietors'[3] of Cardiff, this site had to be given up. When the immigrants next found a plot to their liking, they made sure of getting it by keeping secret their intention to build a church on it. All negotiations were carried on through an Italian layman—Stefano Stavrenghi—one of the few non-Irish Catholics in Cardiff, and it was only when the arrangements for the sale had been carried out and the area of land was securely theirs that the community announced their plans for building a church. The builder from whom the ground had been bought immediately attempted to regain possession of the land but by then it was too late.

These experiences taught the community to tread warily in their dealings with 'outsiders' and nothing was done to provoke opposition to their future building schemes. Thus the log-book of St. Mary's, Canton, shows that when the new school was opened

[1] Cardiff Public Library.
[2] See *Cardiff and Merthyr Guardian*, particularly the issues of 23 April 1842 and 12 January 1861.
[3] Cardiff Diary of the Fathers of Charity, 4 August 1865.

there in 1874 it was opened 'quietly'—presumably to avoid attracting any demonstration of hostility from the residents of Canton.

Abundant evidence of the attitude of the substantial middle class towards the religion of the Irish can be produced but two more examples will be sufficient to illustrate this particular point. In 1848, a riot, described below, occurred in Cardiff during which the Roman Catholic chapel was attacked, but the authorities in control of both the police and the militia took no action either to protect the property of the Irish or to arrest the rioters.² The incident, which was not a small one, was not mentioned in the *Guardian* either. The disregard thus shown for the community's religious susceptibilities was repeated twenty years later at the coming-of-age functions of the young Marquis of Bute, who had been converted to Roman Catholicism. Fr. Signini was invited to the 'County' dinner but was not allowed to speak in case the sight of a Catholic priest delivering a speech offended any of those present. At the workmen's dinner, however, held at the same time, Fr. Clarke, who had been invited, *was* allowed to speak.¹

Hostility to the Irish on religious grounds was supplemented by contempt for them on social grounds. That the Irish were relegated to an inferior status to that of the working class in the town's social structure, is evident from the official reports quoted in Chapter 2. This attitude towards the community was not restricted to local officials, however, as the *Cardiff and Merthyr Guardian* makes clear.

¹ See *The Tablet*: 18 November 1848. An article in this issue signed J.J.B. states that during the riot no action was taken either by the Superintendent of Police or by the magistrates to defend the Irish. There were, apparently, sixty-five soldiers in the town barracks but, although the officer in command placed them under arms immediately he became aware of the outbreak, the civil authorities did not choose to call upon them.

² The story of the 'Welshman's Half-Crown', quoted by the Rev. J. M. Cronin in *St. Peter's Magazine* illustrates the ignorance and superstition concerning Catholicism prevalent among the Welsh working class in the early years of the nineteenth century. John Driscoll, an Irishman living in Cardiff in 1829, was approached by a Welsh workmate who had heard that a Catholic priest visited the town fairly often. The Welshman, having heard lurid stories about such priests, offered Driscoll half-a-crown (a very substantial sum of money for a workman at that time) if the latter would take him to see one. Driscoll, anxious to oblige, arranged for his friend to be present when the visiting priest, a Father Portal, alighted from his coach on his next trip to Cardiff. The Welshman, apparently, departed from the encounter satisfied but disappointed at seeing merely an ordinary human being.

The columns of that paper, during the years between 1848 and 1861 contain frequent references to the behaviour of the Irish in the town, particularly in connection with drunkenness. Whenever 'Paddy' appeared in court, mainly for offences due to over-indulgence in alcohol, the paper treated him as a figure of fun. On 17 March 1849 the *Guardian* recounted with great gusto the story of the 'pretty little unsophisticated Cambrian maiden', recently arrived in Cardiff, who saw some Greek seamen in the street. She was told that they were fierce and uncivilised and exclaimed 'Good gracious, they are quite as bad as the Irish then!'

It was not often, however, that the *Guardian* allowed its attitude towards the Irish to be lightened by humour. The paper took pains to point out to its readers that most of the social evils of the town resulted from the influx of the immigrants and could not be eradicated until the habits of the latter had been changed and their immigration checked.

Hostility to the Irish was not restricted to the classes whose opinions were reflected in the local newspaper; there was strife, also, within the working class itself. The influx of destitute Irish during and after the Famine years, provided local employers with an abundance of cheap labour. The immigrants, in Cardiff as in other parts of the country, were desperate to achieve the means to keep body and soul together and were prepared to accept lower wages and lower living standards than the English or Welsh worker. The inevitable result was 'undercutting' on the part of the Irish and this, in turn, led to bad feeling between them and the native workers, particularly in times of depression in the iron trade. The *Cardiff and Merthyr Guardian* of 21 April 1849, commenting on the abundance of Irish labour at the Cardiff docks, states that 'In consequence of the arrival in this town of swarms of Irish paupers the price of labour has fallen very low: and our native workmen who earn a livelihood among the shipping are almost, if not entirely, beaten out of the market.'

The paper gives examples of the effect of the presence of cheap labour on the native workman. Dock labourers, at that time, were paid 3d a ton for loading and 2½d a ton for wheeling ballast from ships. The Irish workmen offered to do the same work for 1d and

½d a ton respectively. This forced the other workmen to agree to accept these low rates also, whereupon the Irish promptly offered to do the job for ¼d a ton.

Practices of this sort, allied to the fact that the Irish came from a 'foreign' country and practised a religion which was alien to them, provoked considerable hostility amongst the working class. Street brawls between Irish and non-Irish were frequently reported in the local newspaper and conflict of this sort built up feeling to a high pitch. This feeling erupted in the anti-Irish riot of November 1848 mentioned above.

The occasion of the disturbance was the murder by an Irish navvy of a young Welshman named Lewis. The murder took place late at night in Stanley Street, and the Irishman managed to evade capture by the police. The following day, which was a Sunday, passed quietly and Fr. Millea took the opportunity in his evening service to exhort any of his congregation who knew the whereabouts of the culprit or who could assist them in any way to contact the police. This seemed to relieve the tension temporarily.

Early in the afternoon of the following day, three wagon-loads of stones were deposited outside Fr. Millea's house and small groups of people began to congregate in Stanley Street and David Street. By 6 p.m. a crowd of about one thousand gathered outside the priest's house and its leaders claimed that the murderer was concealed inside and threatened to break down the door if they were not admitted in order to search the premises. The priest denied that he had any knowledge of the culprit's identity but said that he was willing to allow the house to be searched by the police and one or two of the mob. Two policemen and three other men accepted the priest's offer and searched every part of the house and church without finding any trace of the man they wanted. The crowd, not satisfied, broke two windows in the church and then moved off and began a systematic attack on the houses of the Irish, breaking doors and windows and destroying furniture.

During this respite, Fr. Millea escaped from the town in disguise and took refuge in a friend's house in the country. After he had gone, the mob, increased in size by this time, assembled once more outside the church and began to attack both it and the priest's

house. All the windows in the church were smashed and great
damage was done to the house, the crowd using as missiles the
stones which had been deposited in the street for that purpose
during the afternoon. After wreaking as much destruction as possible, the mob left the region of the church but still kept control
of the streets, and the area remained in a state of turmoil all
through the following day. Many of the Irish living in the district
left the town in fear of their lives and Fr. Millea, having finally
sought shelter with his Bishop, never returned to Cardiff.

It is reasonable to suppose, from the evidence, that there was
some sort of organisation in this attack on the Irish and that it was
not merely a spontaneous display of fury following the murder of
Lewis. Though this latter event served to bring feeling to a head,
resentment against the Irish, due to the factors mentioned earlier,
had been building up for some time among the labouring classes
and they welcomed the opportunity of giving expression to their
feelings. It is significant that the mob chose to vent their fury on
the church and the priest first of all; they recognised the former
as the symbol of the Irish community and the latter as its visible
head.

The riot of 1848 had long-lasting effects upon the Irish community and was a potent factor in prolonging its isolation throughout the nineteenth century. Public attacks on their religion in the
press, and their relegation by the 'host' society to an inferior social
position had already forced the Irish into a position of some isolation: the incidents of November 1848 convinced the immigrants
both of the depth of feeling against them and of the fact that they
could not rely on the authorities for protection. They needed, then,
to build a community life which would be as self-sufficient as possible and which would reduce contact with the outside world to the
minimum.

There were other factors than that merely of reaction which
made for isolation. The first of these was the physical nature of
the settlement. The description of the Irish settlement previously
given indicates that up to 1861 it was remarkably close-knit. The
first influx of post-Famine Irish concentrated themselves mainly
into the half-dozen streets around St. David's Church, and when

the movement out of this area began the Irish spread only into a district closely linked with the original region of settlement. Not only were the Irish living closely together, however, but the area of Newtown into which most of the immigrants of the years 1850–60 were concentrated was cut off effectively from the rest of the town. Access to Tyndall Street and the streets immediately adjacent to it can only be gained, without inconvenience, from one direction— Bute Street through Herbert Street. The area is bounded on the north by a railway line and on the south by the docks; Bute Street lies to the west, and along the eastern border of the region runs a railway line which can be crossed only by a footbridge or through using a level crossing. This physical isolation, which has endured to the present day, has helped to give point to the general isolation of the community.

During the second half of the nineteenth century the community developed beyond the physical bounds described above, but each successive branch of the settlement founded during those years was situated in an area which was within easy reach of St. David's and it was relatively simple for the Irish in Canton, Grangetown, Splott and Newtown to meet. Until the gradual spread, then, of the Irish into the outlying suburbs and council estates during the years following 1930, the community remained a fairly compact group.

The solidarity of the group was increased by the factors of class kinship and the lack of social mobility. Although a division on the lines of social class has already been noted among the Irish, and a movement of a small section of the community into the economic position of the 'lower-middle' class described, the vast majority of the immigrants reached no higher than the labouring class where they remained throughout the nineteenth century and into the first decades of the twentieth century. There was, then, very little change, during these years, in the internal structure of the community. The reason for this was not merely lack of energy or initiative among the Irish but also the lack of educational facilities for the sons of the immigrants above the level of the elementary schools. By the end of the nineteenth century, the community was well supplied with schools at the lowest level but there was only one school which catered for pupils above the age of 12 or 14 and that was restricted to girls. In 1882 a High School for Catholic boys had been established but this failed through lack of support and was closed before the end of the century.[1] The lack of a Catholic grammar school for boys in the town meant that the chances of the sons and grandsons of the Irish settlers entering the universities and hence the professions were very slight. Thus the tradition whereby the sons of the family left school and took up occupations similar to those held by their father was perpetuated well into the twentieth century; the son's lack of opportunity to 'better himself' acted against the spread of the Irish through the social structure of the town.

The men of the community had not only type of work in common but also, in many cases, place of work. Groups of Irish labourers, often under the supervision of Irish foremen, were to be found in the docks and in the large steel works which was established in Cardiff at the end of the nineteenth century. It became the practice of many of these places for vacancies which were at the disposal of the Irish foreman to be filled by the sons of the community on the personal recommendation of family friends or, frequently, of the parish priest. When no member of the local community was available, news of the prospect of regular work was sent to relatives and friends in Ireland or in other parts of Britain who came to Cardiff as a result and, in many cases, brought their families with them. This practice extended to the supply of teachers for some of the community's schools: the private schools in particular, relied to a large extent on a regular supply of teachers direct from Ireland.[2] The firm of Edward Curran (a medium-sized industrial concern owned by a Catholic family in Cardiff), however, supplies the most striking example of the extension of the community life into the place of work. The founders of the firm felt obliged out of loyalty to the community to draw as much of their labour force as possible from among their fellow Irish-Catholics. There developed, as a result, not only a paternalist

---

[1] Cardiff Diary of the Fathers of Charity, 15 January 1882.
[2] The two convent schools for girls in Cardiff still employ a large number of Irish-born and trained teachers.

relationship between employer and employee but also a heightening of the feeling of kinship between employees themselves. Men working together during the day often met again in the evenings at one or other of the parish meetings or functions. The employees were acquainted with the family histories of their workmates and took an interest in the affairs of the sons and daughters of one another. As recruitment to the firm, until 1939, was carried out mainly by personal recommendation, it was expected that the employee would 'have a word' with the foreman when the time came for his son to leave school and start work, in order to ensure that an opening would be found for him in the firm. In this way, a tradition of employment in Curran's has been built up in many families in the community.

These factors inevitably strengthened the bonds of the community. A position of authority at the place of work conferred upon the holder a measure of prestige in the community so that persons holding responsible jobs often found themselves in demand when the question of filling posts on the committees of the various community organisations came up. The members of the community looked for leadership in their social activities largely to the same people who directed them at their place of work, and in this way the development of a tightly knit group with a recognised hierarchy of prestige was encouraged.

Two more elements important in distinguishing the Irish community from the rest of the people of Cardiff remain to be discussed —the existence of the Ancient Order of Hibernians, and the effect of national sentiment. The former organisation, through its various activities, not only provided the community itself with a social life outside that which came under the direction of the Church—as well as a means to achieve some measure of economic stability—but also provided opportunities for the more ambitious and talented members of the community to fulfil their desires for 'organising' and 'managing'. Those individuals who desired more scope to direct the affairs of their fellows than was provided by the normal parish organisations were able to do so without having to venture beyond the bounds of the community into a society where, they felt, such opportunities may have been denied them. Because of this many of the people who may have played a significant part in breaking down the isolation of the community by taking an active role in affairs outside it, were content to turn their efforts inwards and to contribute to the development of the group's own organisations. By strengthening these organisations they made the community itself less conscious of any need for assimilation with the larger group outside.

The concern of the immigrants for the welfare of their native land was kept alive not only by the events in Ireland down to 1922 but also by the constant influx of new immigrants who could keep them in direct contact with the 'old country'. Another reason for avoiding too much contact with the native population was thus provided—any appearance of losing one's Irish nationality would smack of a disloyalty particularly disgraceful when Ireland was suffering such tribulation.

The influence of the Catholic clergy in deciding the lines along which the Irish community developed and the leading role played by the priests has been emphasised at different points throughout this enquiry. The Irish recognised in the clergy a source of authority far more profound than any outside body, and the word of the priest carried more weight than that of any local official. This reliance upon the clergy as governors, guides and protectors of their affairs removed the members of the community even further away from their fellow-Cardiffians.

A marked sense of solidarity persisted in the Catholic community down to the decade preceding the Second World War. This showed itself in many ways, particularly in the public demonstration on the feast of St. Patrick. During the twenties it was customary for celebrations to spread over three days (in one year, 1925, they lasted a week); St. Patrick's night concerts were held in parish halls throughout the city, a dinner was organised by the Ancient Order of Hibernians and a Grand Irish Concert was held, the biggest cinema in Cardiff being hired for the occasion.[1] The high point of the festivities was reached on the Sunday nearest to St. Patrick's Day when Irishmen from all parts of the city gathered

---

[1] Accounts of the celebrations of the feast of St. Patrick are contained in the March editions of *St. Peter's Magazine* for the years 1920–29.

at a central point and marched in processions, headed by banners and an Irish fife and drum band, numbering, on occasion, as many as five thousand men. Though not a Holiday of Obligation (i.e. a day on which Catholics are obliged to hear Mass), the Masses on St. Patrick's Day were well attended and in many churches shamrock was distributed among the congregation.

Further indications of the strength of the national feeling among the Catholics at this time may be gained from the facts that in 1922 over £1,200 was collected in Cardiff for the Irish Relief Fund[1] (and this at a time when economic conditions were far from good and many of the Irish families were suffering from shortage), and that, at the same time, a Cardiff Irish Fellowship was formed. Also in 1922, a branch of the Gaelic League was founded at St. Peter's and two Irish language classes were formed. Attendance at these was so good that it was hoped that recognition of the subject would be gained from the Cardiff City Council and Gaelic included in the technical section of the education syllabus.

Until the outbreak of the Second World War, then, the Catholic community retained strong characteristics which marked it off from the rest of society in Cardiff, and was conscious of its unity as a group. During the last twenty years, however, a change has taken place which indicates that the Catholics are moving out of their state of isolation. This process will be considered in the last Section of the study.

---

[1] *St. Peter's Magazine*, February 1922. The money was distributed in Cork, Dublin, Belfast and Balbriggan.

# 7. Catholics and Movements directed to Social and Political Reform

The previous Sections of this study have indicated that there were forces working both externally and internally which led to the isolation of urban Catholic communities from society in general. A brief examination of the attitude adopted by Catholics to politics in general and working-class movements in particular will help to illustrate the extent to which they felt themselves to have common interests with their non-Catholic counterparts in the same social class or grouping. This seems an important aspect of the whole question of the process of assimilation which is being undergone by the Catholic minority because support for a 'popular' political or social cause involves the acceptance and sharing of the ideals of those persons or parties which are most active in promoting it. Hence active participation by a substantial number of Catholics in working-class movements would at least show that they identified themselves politically and socially with their non-Catholic counterparts. On the other hand, the acceptance of Catholics into the ranks of the supporters of these movements would indicate a corresponding readiness on the part of non-Catholics to recognise the existence of common ground and mutual interests with them. In this way, the various movements among the working class which were the result of the denial of political rights and bad working and living conditions—which were characteristic of the nineteenth and early twentieth centuries in England and Wales—could have provided powerful forces making for the integration of Catholics into the working class generally.

The opposite also is true. If it can be demonstrated that Catholics did not, in any numbers, participate in these movements and did not, in fact, sympathise with the aims and ideals of those who led them, then Catholics become even further isolated from their fellows. The former share in the social and political benefits won by the efforts of the working class without making any conscious effort to assist in achieving those benefits. What is more important, Catholics do not share in shaping a vital part of working-class tradition and history and, as a result, alienate themselves from becoming a part of the working-class 'way of life' that was to be found in the big towns. This deliberate lack of committal to the causes which were arousing their neighbours in the nineteenth century led to consequences in the twentieth century which will be considered later in the study. What needs to be done first is to indicate some of the reasons for the Catholic attitude towards working-class movements.

In the 1830's, in England, a movement was begun led by a group of workmen the most prominent of whom was James Lovell, a London cabinet maker. This movement was aimed directly at achieving the reform of Parliament and its manifesto contained a number of points including universal manhood suffrage, the payment of members of Parliament and the abolition of property qualifications for members of Parliament. The manifesto was called 'The Worker's Charter' and the members of the movement were dubbed 'Chartists'.[1] It was the aim of the original Chartist leaders to bring pressure to bear on Parliament to achieve reforms which would emancipate the working class politically and which would have the effect of putting into Parliament men from the working class. Such men would, it was felt, understand the needs of their own class and would endeavour to bring about the social reforms which were so badly needed at that time.

It was intended, at first, by the leaders of the movement that peaceable means should be pursued to bring about the ends they were aiming at. They did not contemplate riot and disorder—still less armed rebellion—but relied upon mass meetings in the large towns, monster petitions to Parliament and the columns of their newspaper, *The Northern Star*, edited by an Irishman, Feargus O'Connor, to put their case effectively. This strategy was pursued for some years until, towards the end of the 1830's, the wilder

[1] See Briggs, Asa (ed.) *Chartist Studies* (London, 1959).

spirits among the Chartists grew restless with the lack of results from it and advised more direct action. These individuals—with O'Connor prominent among them—were able to gain control of the movement and the result was a series of riots in various parts of the country including an attempt at armed insurrection in Newport, South Wales, in 1839, led by one John Frost, a former mayor of the town.

The failure of these riots, which were quelled successfully by the authorities, was followed by a sharp decline in the effectiveness of the Chartist movement generally. There were a number of brief revivals of interest in it in the 1840's and a further petition was presented to Parliament demanding the reforms outlined in the Charter, but the movement gradually petered out.

The attitude of the Catholic immigrants to this working-class movement and, in particular, their reaction to the use of violence to achieve its aims, is well demonstrated by the events which occurred in Newport in 1839. John Frost, together with other Chartist leaders from the surrounding towns and villages had planned a march on Newport of several thousand armed workmen. The town was to be taken over by the Chartists and this was to be the signal for uprisings in other parts of Britain with the final aim of bringing down the government of the day and establishing rule based on the Charter. A combination of circumstances, including bad organisation and feeble leadership at the crucial moment, together with the presence in the town of a small troop of soldiers, led to the complete failure of the attempt and some loss of life amongst the attackers.[1] There was a sizeable Irish-Catholic group in Newport at this time and their reactions during the conflict are adequately described in the contemporary newspaper account quoted below.

'The object of the conspiracy (i.e. Chartist revolt) which had spread over extensive districts, was nothing less than the sub-version of the Government, and the establishment of the Chartist system; but the means by which this revolution was to be accomplished—the sacking of small towns and the plunder (if

[1] See Williams, D., *John Frost: A Study in Chartism* (Cardiff, 1939).

not the massacre) of their inhabitants, prove that the population
who could be worked up to peril their lives in such a wild
adventure, must be steeped to the lips in ignorance and almost
as devoid of any reasoning faculty as the beasts of the field—
arising out of these deplorable occurrences there happens to be
one matter of an extremely gratifying nature. It appears that
there is a considerable Irish population in the mining districts,
and that, in consequence of the renumerative price of labour,
those people are comfortably and fully employed. The calum-
niators of the Irish people describe them as habitually prone to
riot, and reckless of all considerations when the temptation to
disturbance is offered. What has been their conduct in Mon-
mouthshire? All along the Irish residents have kept completely
aloof from the Chartists, and although their lives were threatened
the Irishmen refused to have any connexion whatever with the
insurgents. On the contrary a number of them came forward on
the morning of the outbreak to protect the property of their
employers; and (as an Irish paper says) 'it is admitted that the
salvation of Monmouth and the adjoining towns is attributable
to the excellent conduct of our own brave and truly loyal
countrymen.'[1]

The same newspaper goes on to quote the following extract on
the same theme, from the Newport correspondent of a national
journal.[2]

'I have already stated that the Irish, of whom there are large
numbers in this country, steadily refused throughout to be
connected with the Chartist's body, or with the outbreak of last
week. In Newport alone there are upwards of one thousand
Irish workmen—men of that class most likely to be influenced
to join the disaffected here—not two of them, however, did so,
and all the others have not only not exhibited themselves amongst
the ranks of the insurgents, but in the dock-yard, where a large
number of them are employed, upwards of one hundred Irish

[1] Account taken from *The Merlin*, 23 November 1839.
[2] *The Morning Chronicle.*

volunteers assembled on Monday morning last, for the protection of the property there, and of their employers; nay I am aware that several Irish have left this neighbourhood within the last month, declaring that they would be murdered if they remained, because they refused to be connected with the Chartist body. Again, there are thousands of Irish employed in the hills, the hot bed of sedition, and yet not one could be recognised, not one of them had even been suspected of being amongst the rebels who descended on the town last week. . . . The inhabitants of Newport and its neighbourhood have expressed themselves in strong terms of satisfaction as to the conduct of the Irish declaring at the same time, that if they had joined the insurrection, Newport and the adjacent towns must inevitably have been destroyed.'

Opposition to the Chartists on the part of the immigrants was not restricted to this one episode in Newport in 1839. Accounts exist, for instance, of gangs of Irish workmen being organised to break up Chartist meetings in Manchester during the anti-Corn Law campaign in the early 1840's and it was, in fact, due in large part to the activities of the Irish that Manchester Chartism was eventually defeated.[1] Nor was this attitude restricted only to Chartism; the point has been made by several historians that the immigrants took no part in movements for social reform and did not identify themselves with the aspirations of their fellow workmen.[2] If more contemporary evidence of this is needed then the statements of the Rev. Daniel Heane, senior priest at St. Patrick's, Manchester, to the Commission appointed in 1833 to enquire into the employment of children in factories will help.[3] Fr. Heane stated that with another priest, he looked after between 12,000 and 15,000 Catholics, the majority of whom were Irish immigrants. Most of his parishioners worked in factories and lived in the conditions

---

[1] See Read, D., 'Chartism in Manchester' in *Chartist Studies, op. cit.*, and McCord, N., *The Anti-Corn Law League* (London, 1958) pp. 99–103.

[2] See, for example, Redford *op. cit.* and Williams *op. cit.*

[3] *Second Report of the Central Board of His Majesty's Commissioners for inquiring into the Employment of Children in Factories, with Minutes of Evidence, and Reports by the Medical Commissioners*, 1833, evidence of Rev. Daniel Heane, Roman Catholic priest at St. Patrick's, Manchester (p. 14).

already described as typical. After giving these facts, Fr. Heane
made the point specifically that his parishioners did not 'amalga-
mate' with the English work-people at the factory; they did not
readily combine with the other operatives in case of strikes and
generally had to be forced to support any sort of industrial action.

The reasons for this attitude on the part of the immigrants to a
working-class movement aimed at social and political reform are
not far to seek. The origin and background of the Catholic Irish
must first be taken into account. As has already been stated most
of them had lived in Ireland in conditions of indescribable hardship
and suffering and had never known regular employment on a
regular wage. They had been forced to leave their homes and to
look for a means to achieve the basic necessities of life: food,
warmth and shelter. They had been attracted to England because
it offered them not comfort, political rights and social benefits but
the prospect of avoiding a life of semi-starvation. As a result many
of them had made the journey from Ireland, sometimes travelling
as ballast[1] on board the ships which traded regularly between
England and the ports on Ireland's east coast, sometimes coming
as deck passengers on the ships that ran between Dublin and
Liverpool.[2]

Many of those who came this way left relatives or even children
behind living on the little plot of land that was supposed to support
them. The aim was to earn enough in England to pay the rent of
the land in Ireland and to keep alive the hope that one day the
bread-winner could return permanently to build a prosperous life
for himself and his family in his native land. In this connection, a
contemporary writes:

'I myself when in Ireland have seen them return to Ireland from
this country (i.e. Britain); I have seen them in Ireland coming
back; and a man has had the means to pay the rent of his little

[1] See evidence of Medical Officer in *Report to the General Board of Health on
the Town of Cardiff*, (1850).
[2] *Report from the Select Committee on Poor Removal, 1855*, evidence of
J. Corder, p. 14. This witness thought that the Irish had been brought to
Liverpool as deck passengers at 1s or 6d each and that the fare had risen,
by 1855, to 10s each.

patch of ground, namely £3 or £4 or £5, which he has earned in England. I dare say he has begged his way back and has travelled all the way on a mere trifle; but he has saved his money, and in England he has no doubt been living in a very different manner from the English labourer.'[1]

This practice of using funds earned in England to help the people 'back home' had further sides to it. If the emigrants did not come back permanently themselves—and few did—or use their money to support a home in Ireland, they often saved money from their wages in England to send funds home to help others to come over for work. Indeed, it was not uncommon for clubs to be formed —sometimes even among young women—the members of which co-operated to raise sufficient money to send one of their number to England to look for employment. Lots were drawn to decide who should go, and it was then assumed that the fortunate individual would repay his friends by sending money back to help someone else to make the journey.[2]

If all this is taken into account it is not difficult to see at least one of the reasons why the immigrants did not join in the working-class movements. Their lives in England were bounded by the overwhelming desire to get money—and to get it regularly—in order to live and to have something to spare for the people at home. They would not, then, be prepared to forfeit the chance to work by insisting on a certain wage rate and by going on strike to enforce their demands. On the contrary, they were prepared, as we have seen, to accept a lower rate of pay than that demanded by English workmen and thus incurred the stigma of 'blacklegs' or strikebreakers.

This desire to maintain their source of employment and to protect it against what they felt to be the wild and irresponsible activities of their English fellow-workers helps to account for their active opposition to the Chartists during the riots that took place. But another element enters here as well which was of considerable importance at the time; that is, the influence of the Irish Catholic

---

[1] *Report of Select Committee on Poor Removal, 1854,* evidence of R. Pashley.
[2] *Ibid.*

M.P. and leader, Daniel O'Connell. O'Connell, through his constant and successful championship of Irish and Catholic causes—he played a major part in bringing about Catholic Emancipation in 1829—held a position of unique influence both in Ireland and amongst Irish Catholics in England. He had begun by being on friendly terms with Lovell and his working men's association and had sympathised to some extent with the movement. This relationship did not last long, however, and O'Connell, for reasons which will be mentioned later, quickly lost whatever enthusiasm he may have possessed for the cause and began actively to oppose it.[1] Contemporary evidence shows that O'Connell's opposition reached a peak at the time of the 1839 disturbances and he denounced the Chartists violently.

The following extract is taken from a newspaper account of one of O'Connell's speeches.

'Mr. O'Connell has recently fallen foul of the Chartists and made honourable mention of the conduct of some of his poor countrymen, residing in Cardiff, and other towns. England, said Mr. O'Connell, is convulsed to its centre; but the people were foolishly entering into practices involving themselves, that made all good men congregate against them; that was the position of England, with her fiery agitators—the Taylors, the Vincents, the O'Connors. Oh, how I blush for the big O before that name! the first newspaper that I see it in, I shall wet my thumb and rub it out (Laughter). He (Mr. O'Connell) did not make a boast of Irish tranquillity—they knew the Chartists were wrong—they were traitors; and not because Ireland did not feel a sympathy for their distress, but because Irishmen would not obtain advantages through means foul and dishonourable (cheers). Not only in this country did the people of Ireland watch over the friends of Liberty and peace, but in England also. There they attended to the advice of their clergy, who diffused good principles amongst them. In the manufacturing towns in England, the mass of the poor population—not more poor than active—every one of them subsisting on small means—in every one of these

[1] See Halévy, Elie—*A History of the English People in the 19th Century*, vol. III.

towns there was a large garrison of Irishmen. Did they join the Chartists? Did they join the insurrection?

Oh, blessed be God, no. Not only the Irish in Ireland refused to gain any advantage by force, but the Irish in England joined not the Chartists but opposed them, for they only looked for justice by turning the hearts of those who opposed them (cheering). Take the town of Cardiff alone. In that town there were a considerable number of Irish, poor people, who went there to earn their wages in this world, and who endeavoured to procure the means of having a clergyman. . . . What did they do in respect of the Chartist insurrection? Why! 100 of the Irish who had come into the town of Cardiff were sworn in special constables.'[1]

Added, then, to the natural objection of the immigrants to the prospect of their livelihoods being threatened, was the outspoken opposition of the man who had proved himself the most able champion of the Irish-Catholic cause in England. There can be no doubt of O'Connell's personal standing amongst the poor Catholics in the great towns of England, even in the first half of the nineteenth century, when the means of mass communication were not so fully developed to assist in image-building as they are in the twentieth century. 'The Liberator' enjoyed enormous prestige during his own lifetime and became a legendary figure after his death. Considerable weight, then, must be given to the effect of his opposition to a movement like Chartism upon the outlook of Irish Catholics in Britain.

At the same time as he pronounced against the Chartists, O'Connell also came out strongly against the activities of another section of the working-class movement—the trade unions. For a period in the 1820's and 1830's he had shown some sympathy for the union movement amongst the workers, as he had done initially for the working men's association, but his attitude had changed by 1838. In this year a strike occurred at the cotton mills in Glasgow and during it one of the workmen was found murdered. The strikers were immediately accused of causing his death and eighteen

---

[1] Account taken from *The Merlin*, Saturday, 14 December 1839.

of them were arrested. They were charged with conspiracy to intimidate their fellows and conspiring together to take action to secure higher wages. They were found guilty and sentenced to be transported for seven years. The unions reacted violently to the sentence and managed to get twenty thousand signatures to a petition which they presented to Parliament on behalf of the convicted men.[1]

It was at this point that O'Connell came out strongly against the unions. He had been experiencing difficulties with the trade unions in Dublin due basically to the fact that the union's programme of class warfare cut directly across O'Connell's policy of attempting to unite all sections of society in support of the movement towards national emancipation and the repeal of the Act of Union which linked Ireland with England. There was the particular point also that financial support for O'Connell's movement came to a large extent from men in Dublin who were large-scale employers and whose workmen had also gone on strike. These two factors coming together at this time caused O'Connell to decide to take a firm line and he delivered a speech in Parliament in which he denounced what he called the 'criminal outrages' committed by the union members. He went further than this and condemned generally all 'secret societies' adding the complaint that the anarchy which he said was prevailing in Ireland made it impossible for judge and jury to convict and punish the guilty parties.[2]

It is clear, then, that at a crucial point in the development of those causes with which the working class identified themselves during the nineteenth century, the Irish urban Catholics decided that it was in their interests not only to stand aloof from them but actively to oppose them, and that they were confirmed in this decisions by the actions and eloquence of the one man who exercised indisputable influence over them.[3] Another factor, then, was introduced to isolate them from their environment and to cause a rift between them and their fellows in the working class. The

[1] See Halévy *op. cit.*, pp. 293ff.
[2] *Ibid.*
[3] See H. U. Faulkner, 'Chartism and the Churches' in Rosenblatt, F. F., Slosson and Faulkner—*The Social and Economic Aspects of the Chartist Movement* (New York, 1916).

hostile indifference thus shown to that area of English politics which affected them as a social class was not, however, an indication that Irish Catholics were politically inactive. They were, in fact, very active but the field in which they expressed themselves provides the final reason for their 'separation' from their immediate environment; for what the immigrants were mainly interested in was Irish politics and that, in turn, meant the achievement of Home Rule for Ireland.

The second half of the nineteenth century witnessed the beginning of the Fenian movement in Ireland, for in 1858 the Irish Republican Brotherhood had been formed in Dublin. This particular organisation was distinguished by the fact that it had adopted the republican ideals of Wolfe Tone and aimed at achieving national independence. The members of the Brotherhood were prepared to use force if necessary. The movement had grown to such strength in 1865 that an armed uprising was planned; this eventually took place in 1867 but proved to be a failure and resulted in the capture and imprisonment of many of the Fenian leaders. In spite of this setback, however, the Fenian movement continued to flourish and it played an important part in the Irish struggle for independence right down to the achievement of Home Rule in 1922.

Fenian sympathisers were to be found in many of the Irish communities in the industrial towns of Britain and a number of the immigrants were at first prepared to take an active part in helping the movement. This was illustrated by the attempt in 1867 to blow up the wall of Clerkenwell prison in order to release Fenian prisoners inside, and by the case of the 'Manchester Martyrs'— three young Irishmen who were executed for their part in an attempt to rescue two Fenian prisoners. In other towns there were symptoms of unrest and disturbance among the Irish population, particularly at the time of the 1867 rising in Ireland, and the clergy were sometimes called upon by the authorities to exercise their influence to prevent any open outbreaks of violence.[1]

[1] For example in Cardiff, where the priests were reported in 1867, as carrying out 'negotiations' with the Fenian leaders in order to allay public uneasiness (Cardiff Diary of the Institute of Charity).

This interest in Irish politics among the Catholic community throughout Britain became of supreme importance during the last two decades of the nineteenth century. The formation of a new party which was dedicated to achieving legislative independence for Ireland from the Imperial Parliament at Westminster signalled the rise of a new movement in politics which resulted in bringing together Catholic voters all over Britain. The Irish Nationalist leaders were fully aware that the majority of Catholics in Britain were Irish or of Irish descent and they made every effort to exploit that fact; the 'Catholic vote' was thus organised in a way it had never been before to support the movement for Home Rule in Ireland.

This development was further stimulated by events which occurred in the 1880's. In 1878 an agrarian movement called the Land League was launched in Ireland by an Irishman called Michael Davitt, a man who had had experience of life and work in a factory town in Lancashire. A few years later this political association, with some modifications, was introduced into England by T. P. O'Connor. In England the organisation was known as the United Irish League and was to become the major Irish party in the cities and towns throughout the land. From this time on, until the achievement of Ireland's independence in 1922, Catholics in England were at last aroused by a political movement which they could take as being entirely their own. By expressing their patriotism for Ireland and supporting the Home Rule movement they could take part in politics without having to co-operate with the native workers. They had a common cause to unite them and support for that cause was given a certain appeal for the fact that they felt it to be in the face of opposition from their non-Irish neighbours.

This sense of Catholics working together against 'the rest' was increased by the fact that when the Catholic vote was mustered on a question of internal politics it was invariably on an issue

---

In Merthyr Tydfil, a town in South Wales with a considerable immigrant Irish community, the Roman Catholic priest felt it necessary to hold an 'anti-Fenian' meeting after Mass (see *The Merlin*, 11 January 1868).

which directly affected their own vital interest as a religious group. The most enduring of these issues has been the struggle to maintain the rights of the Catholic community in the sphere of education. In 1884 Bishop Vaughan of Salford made what was probably the first comprehensive attempt to organise Catholic opinion on a domestic issue in English politics when he founded the voluntary schools association. This organisation was aimed at enlisting the support and concentrating the voting power of the Catholic electorate on efforts to remedy the disabilities under which the Church's schools were suffering as a result of the prevailing educational policy of the government.

This concentration of Catholic political effort on the question of Catholic schools has persisted down to the present day.[1] Politically it has resulted in a considerable measure of success for the Catholic 'cause' but it has also had its own effects both upon the Catholic's view of his role in English politics and on the view that the remainder of the electorate tend to take of Catholics as a political force. On the one hand, the Catholic brought up in the tradition already described in the early part of this study is liable to regard his duty in politics as being restricted to achieving what is in the best interests of his own community. He is encouraged in this view by the continued efforts of the clergy to focus attention on the schools issue and by the tendency of the Catholic journals to highlight issues of 'Catholic' interest. On the other hand, and as a result of this sectional approach to questions of the day, the remainder of the electorate tend to look upon Catholics as members of a political 'pressure group' unconcerned with questions which affect society as a whole but prepared to go into brisk and effective action when their own interests are involved.

Valiant efforts have been made during the whole period under study, by Catholics both individually and in groups, to break out of this narrow approach and to involve themselves and their co-religionists in the great social and political issues of their time. Individual Catholics can, for example, be found in the ranks of the Chartists (the author's namesake being the one Irishman who joined

---

[1] For a full discussion of the history of the struggle for Catholic schools see the works on Catholic Education quoted in the Bibliography.

in the riot at Newport—on the side of the rioters)[1] and amongst the
Trade Unionists, and it is revealed that one Catholic priest attended
meetings of the leaders of the Chartists in the North-Midlands.[2]
The most famous and prominent of these exceptions is, of course,
Cardinal Manning. Manning—like Newman, and perhaps signi-
ficantly, a convert—was concerned throughout his entire life with
the principles of social justice. His deep and abiding interest in the
affairs of the poor and underprivileged was manifest from the time
of the beginning of his career as an Anglican clergyman, years
before he was received into the Catholic Church and he expressed
himself clearly and vigorously both in speech and in writing on the
necessity of translating Christian social principles into positive
action on behalf of those sections of the population suffering from
want or distress.[3]

Manning himself was prepared to set a personal example in this,
and the most famous occasion when he did so was when he inter-
vened in the London dock strike of 1889. By using his personal
influence and prestige the Cardinal was able to obtain concessions
from the employers which were accepted by the men on strike
when Manning met them at their own headquarters. This action
'lit up as with a splendid, contrasting, solitary flare the long waste
of his Catholic contemporaries' general indifference to the question
of social rights',[4] but no school of enthusiasts was left to carry on
work in this sphere and only the memory of his abiding concern
for social justice remained. For even Manning was compelled to
concede that Irish politics were the chief concern of his flock and
to submit to that state of affairs as being not only inevitable
but correct. In 1890, for instance, we find him writing
ruefully:

[1] See Williams, D., *op. cit.*, Patrick Hickey was the only Irishman in Newport
to take the Chartist oath.

[2] He was the Rev. Thaddens O'Malley who was elected as a delegate from
Nottingham to the Chartist national assembly which met in London on 1 May
1848 (see Faulkner, H. U., 'Chartism and the Churches', *op. cit.*).

[3] For an account of this aspect of Manning's career and outlook see Fitzsimons,
J. (ed.) *Manning: Anglican and Catholic* (London, 1951), particularly the section
by Fitzsimons, J., 'Manning and the Workers'. See also McLelland, V. A.,
*Cardinal Manning: His Public Life and Influence 1865–92* (London, 1962),
particularly for Manning's social and educational policy.

[4] Rev. P. Hughes in *The English Catholics*, *op. cit.*

'Once it was my fate to ask the people at St. Mary's to sign a petition to Parliament. The petition lay for signature in the school next to my house. I found that a young Irishman had emptied the ink-bottle over it as a protest against Parliament.'[1]

Perhaps it was an accumulation of experiences such as this that led Manning in his later years to write to the Bishops in Ireland assuring them that he recognised as a fact that the achievement of justice and liberation for Ireland should be the first concern of the immigrant Catholics in the sphere of politics and that he would do nothing to distract them from this cause.[2]

After Manning's death, and during the first two decades of the twentieth century, attempts were made in certain areas of England to organise action among Catholics on social questions. In the diocese of Salford, for example, between 1906 and 1909 an organisation was formed known as the Salford Diocesan Federation which aimed at co-ordinating the efforts of clergy and laity under the leadership of the bishops and of training Catholics for active participation in politics in whatever party they chose to join. This was regarded as a solution to the problem of organising Catholic influence upon contemporary English life. The practical use of the Federation, however, was more or less destroyed by the perennial influence of the Irish question. In 1908 the Liberal candidate at a by-election in North-West Manchester—an area where there was an important Catholic vote—was defeated and a powerful group of the local Irish pro-Liberal politicians blamed the Federation, rightly or wrongly, for their candidate's defeat. The result was much bitter feeling and the paralysis of organised Catholic action for years to come.[3]

The Federation lasted for nearly twenty years after this date and published a monthly review, *The Catholic Federationist*. One of the organisation's earliest activities was the persistent lobbying at the

[1] *Ibid.*
[2] See Gwynn, D., 'Manning and Ireland' in *Manning: Anglican and Catholic* (*op. cit.*), also McClelland, V. A., *op. cit.* McClelland states that Manning subordinated all questions, even that of education, to that of the cause of Ireland. He wished the latter to be the foremost concern of Catholics in England (p. 188).
[3] See *The English Catholics, op. cit.*

Labour party conferences to secure the deletion from the agenda of
the clause demanding secular education in the public elementary
schools; in this the Catholic group was ultimately successful.
During this same period there also developed an organisation
known as the National Conference of Catholic Trade Unionists,
which for a long time played a large part in the struggle to keep the
Labour party a non-socialist body. In 1918, when the Labour
party 'socialised' its constitution the National Conference came to
an end.

It is significant that in both these attempts to involve Catholics
in English politics the task was regarded as being that of exerting
'Catholic influence' on current affairs and of bringing Catholic
pressure to bear on the Labour party to mould its constitution in a
way that would be acceptable to current Catholic thinking. However well-intentioned the efforts may have been, the activities of
both the Federation and the National Conference of Catholic Trade
Unionists would be regarded by those outside as further evidence
of the struggle of a pressure group to exert influence for its own
ends and as further evidence of the separateness of the Catholic
group from its non-Catholic environment.

The settlement in Ireland in 1922 finally removed the main
political 'target' for the immigrant Catholics. Attempts have been
made since 1922 to fill the gap thus caused by making Catholics
fully active in English politics and two main lines of approach have
been tried. On the one hand there has been the persistence of the
idea that groups should be formed as and when the 'Catholic
interest' demanded it; in 1945, for instance, after the Butler Education Act of 1944 and before the General Election which followed
the end of the war with Germany, the 'Catholic Parents and
Electors Association' was formed, with branches in the major
towns of England and Wales. The immediate purpose of this
organisation was to ensure that Parliamentary candidates would be
approached and asked for their views on the 1944 Education Act
and the provisions it made for Catholic schools. At the same
time, the candidates were to be made aware of Catholic feeling
on the matter and to draw whatever conclusions they thought
fit.

The other approach, adopted notably by the Catholic Social Guild, has been to prepare Catholics to participate in political and social action by instructing them in the social doctrines of the Catholic Church. The main sources for these doctrines have been found in the encyclicals of the Popes, beginning with the *Rerum Novarum* in 1891 and culminating in the writings of Pope John XXIII. The Catholic Social Guild have established branches in many of the major towns in Britain, have founded the Catholic Workers College (re-named Plater Hall after its founder) at Oxford, have issued a great number of books and pamphlets and have generally worked very hard to interest Catholics in their social duties and at the same time, to persuade non-Catholics that the Catholic Church can provide the principles upon which society can be formed. The fact that this tremendous effort has met with only moderate success in the past and that support for it is becoming increasingly difficult to find at the present time seems to be related to two basic considerations—apart, that is, from the effects that powerful forces of social change are having on urban Catholics generally, a factor which will be examined in the final section of this study. First of all, as far as their co-religionists themselves were concerned the Guild have had to contend with the long tradition of indifference to political and social questions which has been the inheritance of many adult Catholics today. This has been a formidable barrier and it may perhaps be arguable that an attempt to instil into students a body of social doctrine which at first sight —because of the high level of abstraction of the thought and the 'difficult' language in which it was expressed—was not immediately applicable to the affairs of the day, was not the best way to overcome it.

The second consideration comes into play when the effort to persuade non-Catholics—trade unionists, active politicians and the ordinary electorate—that the Catholic Church can provide basic principles upon which to found and operate society is examined. Here the Guild have not only to overcome the hostility caused by the opposition of Catholics to movements among the workers for social and political reform but have also to combat a long-standing divorce from organised religion which has become part of the urban working-class 'way of life'.[1] Right from the start of large-scale urbanisation in Britain in the eighteenth century the working classes, the labouring poor, the artisan class, as a class and as adults have been kept out of the protestant churches. There were a number of reasons for this. To begin with there was the simple fact of lack of space for them in the church buildings themselves; the system of 'seat rents' or payment for pews, meant that those who could not afford the money to pay could not go to church. True there were a number of 'free' seats in each church but these were invariably awkwardly placed and few in number. Then there were class differences. The squalid material conditions in which the workers existed and their own way of life bound them into a pattern of life that made them appear as foreigners when they were compared with their more affluent and hence more stable and 'respectable' fellow townsmen. This in turn made them content with their own exclusion; they had no wish to worship with others who were not in their class and who were prepared to bestow on them the humiliation of relegating them to the least convenient seats in the church.

There were large-scale social factors also that were operating to encourage the separation between organised religion and the working class. The poor have always existed but until urbanisation they were a recognisable section *within* the community. As the population grew, however, the poor became an undifferentiated group which was lost to sight except as a mass. At the same time there was the economic rise of a 'middle class' which was becoming, in the nineteenth century, increasingly religious in its habits and the combination of the two social phenomena resulted in a social stratification in which religious and denominational lines ran parallel to the economic so that the poor were excluded both socially and religiously. This in turn hardened the separation of the classes and widened the gulf between the churches and the working classes.

[1] The analysis which follows is based largely on the work of E. R. Wickham in *Church and People in an Industrial City* (London, 1957). Bishop Wickham's conclusions are supported by the evidence of his study in Sheffield and the works dealing with the Churches and the working classes quoted in the Bibliography. A vivid illustration of the divorce between worker and organised religion is provided, albeit in novel form and at first hand, by Tressall, R., in *The Ragged Trousered Philanthropists*, London, 1914.

A combination of all these social and economic factors brought into being a positive social and political re-orientation of the working class into a direction of its own. In the twentieth century a strong positive and solid working-class pattern of life has been set and the practice of religion is not part of this pattern. The material struggle to exist has made the consideration of religion seem irrelevant; it appears essentially as a refinement or a luxury. Having built their society without the help of the Church or without religion playing a meaningful part of its construction, it is hard to see how members of the working classes can be expected at this stage to see the Church in the role of a leader in social and political reform.

Since the end of the Second World War in 1945, there have been considerable changes in the position of urban Catholics in society. These changes will be treated in more detail in the next section but it is appropriate to note here some of the changes in 'political' outlook in the Catholic Church. At the same time as there has been a continuation of the policy of forming special Catholic groups for 'political' ends, e.g. the Catholic Parents and Electors Association already mentioned and the Association of Catholic Trade Unionists —there has been a growing emphasis on the fact that Catholic Action generally must have its base firmly in society. That is to say that the most effective way that a Catholic solicitor, doctor, miner, labourer or trade unionist can bear Christian witness is to be first an efficient solicitor, doctor, miner, labourer or trade unionist; committal to and mastery of the actual trade or profession undertaken is advocated as being the first duty of a Christian in society. This idea had not been extended to the sphere of politics until very recently. In the last two years in conferences and lectures and in the pages of a new Catholic review a small group of young Catholic intellectuals—clerical and lay—have been forcefully advocating the idea that there must be among Catholics a practical committal to and involvement in internal national politics.[1] This must not be in the sense of forming a Catholic group on the old model, aimed at watching over 'Catholic interest' or self-consciously attempting to

[1] This view is put forward strongly by, in particular, T. Eagleton in the issues of *Slant* in 1965.

introduce 'Catholic' principles into politics, but must take the form of a personal involvement in local or national politics on the same basis as the non-Catholic comrade in arms. The point is continually made that if a Catholic is seriously concerned about social or political reforms then he must become an active member of a political group that is striving to achieve those reforms and not think that he can influence events from outside.

As has been stated earlier there have always been individual Catholics who have played an active part in internal politics and there are a handful of Catholic members of Parliament today. What there has not been before is a Catholic journal which urges its reader to espouse radical causes for their own sake and to consider themselves as something less than Christians if they don't. It is not easy to say at this stage what effects—positive and negative—this line of action may have, both on the Catholics who are reached by these views and on the manner in which Catholics generally are regarded as 'political animals' by those outside the Church. But the fact that such a group of young Catholics not only exists but can produce a journal to act as a mouthpiece for their views is itself an indication that change is taking place and takes its place in the evolution of Catholicism in England today.

A postscript must be added to this section for at no point in it has the political significance of the old Catholics been considered. It may be stated at once that the members of this part of Catholicism in England as described in Chapter 1 have done little or nothing to alter the picture already painted of a Catholic group divorced from internal politics and being aroused only by events which affected its own interest. Although at first sight the old Catholics may have appeared to have been suited by wealth and social status to give some sort of leadership to the urban Catholic masses, they were in fact precluded from doing so by a number of factors. To begin with, as mentioned in Chapter 1, the old Catholics had no bond of sympathy and little of interest with their urban co-religionists, and they had, in many cases, an active dislike for the movement for Home Rule for Ireland and a distaste for its leaders.[1] The attitude

---

[1] The attitude of the Catholic aristocracy towards O'Connell was roundly condemned in 1830 by William Cobbett. Writing in *The Political Register* (vol. 70, p. 120) under the form of a letter to O'Connell, Cobbett says:

of many of the Catholic peerage towards O'Connell and his
championship of the Irish cause was ambivalent to say the least,
and a number of the prominent converts to Catholicism—including
Newman himself—regarded O'Connell with suspicion and dislike.[1]

It has to be remembered in this connection also that as these
Catholics had only been re-admitted to society in the first part of
the nineteenth century, after a long period of persecution and
political exile, they could not be expected to possess the habit of
political and social action. Newman says in 1852:

'Robbed, oppressed and thrust aside, Catholics in these islands
have not been in a condition for centuries to attempt the sort of
education which is necessary for the man of the world, the
statesman, the landholder or the opulent gentleman. . . . Their
legitimate stations, duties, employments, have been taken from
them, and the qualifications withal, social and intellectual which
are necessary both for reversing the forfeiture and for availing
themselves of the reversal.'[2]

If the 'upper-class' English Catholic was thus disabled from
exercising his powers on matters of great moment to the society in
which he lived, where did he find the opportunity to express himself politically? Again, as with the urban Catholic, the answer was
on an issue of 'Catholic' interest. During the third quarter of the
nineteenth century the most pressing question for Catholics was
the long conflict between Pope Pius IX and the King of Sardinia
which resulted from the latter's attacks on the Church and on the
papal states. This was not the remote, academic problem it would
appear at first sight, for England, perhaps more than any other non-
Italian country in Europe, except France, was actively interested in

---

'Your cause is the cause of talent and generosity and gratitude; and the day is,
I am sure, not far distant, when your base abandoners will, if you pursue the
proper course, tremble at the sound of the name of O'Connell, and when men,
being at a loss for a simile where with to crown the climax of hellish ingratitude,
will think of the Catholic aristocracy of England and Ireland.'

[1] In his *Apologia Pro Vita Sua* (*op. cit.*, p. 191) Newman notes: 'I had an
unspeakable aversion to the policy and acts of Mr. O'Connell, because as I
thought he associated himself with men of all religions and no-religions against
the Anglican Church, and advanced Catholicism by violence and intrigue.'

[2] Quoted by Rev. P. Hughes in *The English Catholics*, *op. cit.*

the Italian revolution, and this interest had a strongly anti-papal bias. The issue became one of domestic politics in Britain and it occupied newspaper columns for years. The status of the Pope was involved and Catholics found themselves the sole supporters of his cause as far as public speech and action were concerned. A succession of Whig-Liberal governments in England encouraged Victor Emanuel in his course of action until, in 1859–60, the revolution was successfully accomplished. The most prominent of the old Catholics were intensely preoccupied with this question and devoted time and energy to it rather than to internal political affairs.

With the urban Catholics concentrating upon Irish affairs and Catholic questions and the old Catholics unfitted by tradition or inclination to lead them into playing an active role in internal politics in England, a picture is built up of Catholics separating themselves from their neighbours in the sphere of politics. That this isolation was chosen and deliberate, at least on the part of the urban immigrants, seems clear from the evidence of their attitude towards movements for social and political reform, and the effects of this, in turn, have meant that Catholics have played little part in shaping a vital element in the working-class tradition and way of life. Some of the consequences of this have already been mentioned: more will be examined in the next section.

# 8. Catholics and urban society, 1965

The isolation of the urban Catholic groups was the result of a combination of factors which have already been examined. The presence of these factors has been noted as being general throughout the urban areas, and the detailed examination of Cardiff has shown how they operated in practice. The external pressures, rising mainly from religious practice and social discrimination, exerted by the host society on the immigrant group helped to bring about the initial separation of Catholics from their social environment, and this preliminary cleavage was made deeper by the force of reaction on the part of the newcomers against hostility from outside.

Separation was prolonged, however, by forces working within the Catholic community itself. Briefly, these may be said to be related to the elements of religion and nationality. Membership of the Roman Catholic Church provided the immigrants with the means by which their lives could be organised on the basis of a community with its own institutions, and the Roman Catholic priesthood provided a regular supply of ready-made and acceptable leaders. It was thus possible for a pattern of life to be developed amongst Catholic groups which was, to a considerable extent, independent of the larger society within which they were situated.

The national origin of the urban Catholics, as the previous chapter has shown, meant that this separation spread into the field of politics, so that, generally speaking, Catholics in England and Wales did not show much sympathy for—and on a number of occasions actively opposed—the movements for political and social reform which developed among their fellow-workers. Hence, not only was one possible path to assimilation firmly blocked, but the antipathy aroused among the larger working-class society by these political activities—or lack of them—helped to emphasise still further the divisions which already existed.

157

The indications are that the isolation of the urban Catholic groups in England and Wales is being broken down and that the process has been continuing with increasing rapidity since the end of the Second World War. It will be the purpose of this final section to isolate a number of the main reasons for and symptoms of what appears to be a growing assimilation of urban Catholics into their social environment and to attempt an analysis of the process on the lines of those conducted on the stages of assimilation through which other minorities—in England and the United States of America—have passed. Briefly, the factors which have emerged during the study as being mainly responsible for the isolation of Catholics have fallen roughly into three categories—religious, social and national. It is not easy, as has been demonstrated, to separate out these categories because often two or all of them have combined to produce a single result and so it must be emphasised once more that if they are treated in isolation it is only because in this way some analysis becomes possible. It must also be admitted at this point that the evidence which indicates 'assimilation' on the part of Catholics with the larger society is 'negative' rather than 'positive'; that is to say that it is to be found more in the breaking-up of an old way of life which symbolised a Catholic group than in indications that Catholics are consciously attempting to move out of a state of isolation. This lack of positive evidence may be the result of the fact that insufficient basic research has yet been done to reveal its existence, or it may be the result of quite other factors, some of which will be mentioned later.

The decline in importance of the 'nationalistic' factor is perhaps the first and most obvious point to note. The granting of independence to most of Ireland in 1922 removed a political cause but it did not immediately destroy a nationalistic identification amongst urban Catholics. The large-scale demonstrations connected with the feast of St. Patrick, for instance, continued in many places during the 1920's and into the years immediately preceding 1939 and community organisations like the Ancient Order of Hibernians and the Gaelic League also flourished during the same period. The Masses on St. Patrick's Day itself were well-attended and shamrock was still often distributed in the churches. By 1965 all this had

changed. In the large urban areas with substantial numbers of
Catholics there is still some sort of celebration on St. Patrick's Day
—normally a dance—but nothing on the pre-war scale with processions, banners and bands of Irish pipes. The Masses on
St. Patrick's Day are not now distinguished by congregations
much larger than for a normal weekday and the organisations like
the Gaelic League and the Ancient Order of Hibernians are practically defunct. The Irish Anti-Partition League still draws a
nominal amount of support but it comes mainly from the older of
the Irish-born Catholics, i.e. those who arrived in this country
when the political troubles in Ireland were reaching their peak.
Young immigrants nowadays find the 'social' activities of this
organisation useful when they first arrive. They meet their fellow-
Irish at them and can enjoy the occasional 'ceilidh', so that the
shock of transition to a strange environment is cushioned. Once
they have accustomed themselves to the change, however, have
settled into a job and, perhaps, married and set up a home, these
newcomers tend to lose interest in the 'League' and find the extreme
nationalism and tendencies to dwell in the past of some of its
members distasteful.

It is only by the handful of extreme nationalists amongst the
Catholic body that it is considered 'unpatriotic' to be unconcerned
about the wrongs of Ireland, and it is no longer felt necessary to
hold parades to demonstrate fervour for the 'old country'. As a
result, the descendants of the immigrants are no longer constantly
reminded of their 'national' heritage and urged to remember the
distinction between themselves and the British. Outside the urban
areas of South Lancashire, the sight of a procession of men wearing
the green, white and gold and headed by a pipe and drum band
would be quite unfamiliar to a child born after 1939 and would
only be a dim childhood memory for the generation born between
1920 and 1930.

As an external factor making for isolation, religious hostility to
Catholics has declined considerably in importance. This development springs from a number of causes of which three may be
mentioned. To begin with there appears now to be a widespread indifference and apathy towards religion on the part of the

population.[1] The roots and causes of this attitude would require a separate series of studies to elucidate but its presence helps to reduce the likelihood of religious prejudice operating as a divisive factor in society.

Then there is the fact that the Roman Catholic Church with a regular hierarchical structure has been established in England and Wales for over one hundred years and has become a familiar institution; familiarity, in this case, has helped to breed acceptance. Prejudice in the past—as the quotations earlier in the study show—was based largely on fear of the Church and ignorance of its workings, but the descendants of the burgesses of 1826 who were exhorted not to yield up their Bibles no longer seem to regard the Roman Catholic Church as a sinister organisation and it is doubtful if the working man of today, accustomed to seeing priests every day in the streets, would be prepared to pay half-a-crown for the privilege.[2] Finally, during recent years and particularly since the Second Vatican Council began, there has been an increasing emphasis amongst Catholics on active co-operation with non-Catholic Christians and there has been a positive response from most of the latter. The significance of this last factor as a means of overcoming religious hostility in the population generally is difficult to estimate and should not be over-stressed, applying, as it does, to active non-Catholic Christians who constitute a relatively small proportion of the total population. Nevertheless, the combination of all three causes has resulted in the Catholic being relieved of the necessity of being continually on the defensive and watchful of his relationships with non-Catholics.

The Catholic urban communities have also benefited, together with the working class generally, from the improved economic conditions which have existed since the last war; consequently they have been able to share in the increased opportunities for social mobility and have risen from their position as a depressed class.

[1] Cf. Marsh, D. C. *The Changing Social Structure of England and Wales, 1871–1951* (London, 1958). He quotes figures (p. 187) which indicate that in 1951 there was a total membership of the Protestant Churches (including the Quakers) in England and Wales of 4,810,100, *i.e.* slightly more than 10 per cent of the total population.

[2] See Chapter 6.

Unfortunately it is not yet possible to speak in anything but general terms of the extent to which Catholics have become upwardly mobile. No detailed information is available relating to their progress in this respect as a group. The results of a survey carried out in a small town in England and published in 1953 showed that at that time of all the religious denominations studied—Anglican, Nonconformist and Roman Catholic—only the Roman Catholic and the Brethren had membership drawn almost exclusively from occupational class C.[1] This serves as an indication that Catholics as a body have not yet caught up, in terms of social rising, with non-Catholics. This does not mean, however, that they still occupy the lowest social positions. Their economic position has improved, and the effect of this change in economic status has been heightened by the improvement in educational facilities available for Catholic youth. A substantial network of Catholic grammar schools has been built up throughout England and Wales in the first half of the twentieth century, thus providing an opportunity for the sons of the immigrants to benefit from the type of education which could lead them into the universities and professions.

During the years prior to 1939, when the bulk of the Catholic population belonged to the poorer section of society, and when a grammar school education for their children could still be beyond the pockets of many parents with large families, this educational development did not affect more than a small proportion of children. Exactly what that proportion was it is not possible to say as statistics do not exist on which to base an estimate. Even if the gross total of pupils attending Catholic grammar schools in any one year prior to 1945 were to be collected it still would not provide a reliable indication as many of these schools contained a substantial proportion of non-Catholic pupils. Also, it is not possible to estimate how many Catholic pupils were attending non-Catholic grammar schools. Some progress has been made to

---

[1] There has been very little research done yet into the social mobility of Catholics. The indications are, however, that, as has been said, the 'movement up' of Catholics is of recent date; Catholics are not now a depressed class but they still were, in 1953, prominent in Group C of the occupational gradings. See Bottomore, T. 'Social Stratification in Voluntary Organizations' in Glass, D. V. (ed.), *Social Mobility in Britain* (London, 1954).

overcome this first difficulty in measurement, but the second
obstacle still remains and so it is possible only to speak in general
terms of social mobility as affected by increased educational
opportunity.[1]

During the war years, 1939–45, when economic conditions
improved, grammar school education for their children was
brought within the reach of a larger proportion of parents and
the numbers in the Catholic schools increased accordingly. This
increase was further stimulated by the introduction of free
grammar school education in 1944, and when the system of
university grants and scholarships was enlarged and extended,
university education came within the reach of many more children.
The result has been that a steady trickle of children whose parents
are descendants of the original Irish-Catholic settlers has passed
from the grammar schools to the universities and from the universities have entered the professions. This has meant that boys
whose parents and grandparents were occupied in labouring work
or manual trades have moved out of this sphere of activity and can
be found in all professions—medicine, law, teaching, accountancy
—working alongside colleagues whose backgrounds differ from
their own. In this way the sense of solidarity among the urban
Catholic groups is being weakened; these is less sense of community of interest between the generation born between 1920 and
1940 and that of its parents than there was between previous
generations; wider loyalties are being formed and the present-day
descendants of the immigrants are to be found in most levels of
the social structure. The increasing opportunities for the generation born in 1930 and later to be socially mobile has meant that
there is a difference in the rate of assimilation between representatives of these generations and their parents and grandparents.

Perhaps the most important single factor in hastening the
assimilation of Catholics has been the effect of the war of 1939–45.
During the war young men from all the urban Catholic groups left
their homes to join the armed services and hence became immedi-

[1] Cf. Matthijssen, M. A. J. M., 'Catholic intellectual emancipation in the
Western countries of mixed religion' (*Social Compass*, vol. VI, no. 3). A good
account—though now somewhat out of date—of some of the difficulties in this
sphere is contained in this article.

ately exposed to a much wider sphere of contacts than they had experienced at home. The First World War, however, must have had a similar effect—though restricted to a smaller circle of men—yet the period immediately following 1918 witnessed no spectacular decline in the unity of community life. But there are essential differences between the two periods. In 1918 the struggle for independence in Ireland was moving towards its climax—the famous Easter rebellion had taken place in 1916—and there was still a powerful national sentiment to help bind Catholics together. This was not the case in 1945. Another important factor was the far greater direct participation of the civilian population in the second war than in the first. This participation, involving the presentation of a united front to the danger of air attack—to mention only one aspect—meant that all sections of the civilian society had to join together, regardless of distinction of class or society, to face a common enemy.

Other factors remain to be mentioned. Intermarriage between Catholic and non-Catholic is one obvious means of encouraging the assimilation of Catholics into their environment, but how widespread and frequent this practice has been it is not yet possible to say with any certainty.[1] There is also the fact of the break-up of the physical unity of the urban Catholic groups which are being affected by the same social pressures in this direction as other working-class groups.[2] Original areas of settlement in the industrial towns are becoming depopulated—or, at least, have a shifting population—as the younger families move out to housing estates—public and private—on the fringes of the cities. The splintering effect of such movements is being counteracted, to some extent, by the formation of new parishes in the outlying districts and, in some cases, the

---

[1] The uncertainty arises from the lack of reliable published statistics covering the whole country.

[2] For summaries of the forces affecting these social groups see: Marsh, D. C., *op. cit.*, and Cole, G. D. H., *Studies in Class Structure*, (London, 1955).

For more detailed research, see for example, Bott, E. *Family and Social Network* (London, Tavistock Publications). Townsend, P. *The Family Life of Old People* (London, 1957). Thomason, G. F. 'The Effects of Industrial Changes on Selected Communities in South Wales' (University of Wales Ph. D. Thesis, Cardiff, 1963); and *Neighbourhood and Community* (University of Liverpool Press, 1954).

setting-up of parish schools so that the basis is hopefully laid for
the formation of separate sub-communities. Recent research is
showing, however, that the formation of a parish does not auto-
matically mean the creation of a community—a point to which we
shall return later—and meaningful links between individuals are
suffering from the geographical 'explosion' of the old settlements.
As the housing estates retreat further and further from the centres
of the cities, contact between children who have left their old sur-
roundings and parents and grandparents who have remained
inevitably becomes more difficult and is reduced in frequency.[1]
The man of the family, also, can only retain contact with his old
friends when they share the same place of work. Inevitably, the
husband-wife-children relationship, together with place of work,
become increasingly important as the basis of social life.[2]

Studies of minorities, both racial and religious, and analyses of
the manner in which they have become assimilated into the larger
society in which they are situated, have provided a useful instru-
ment with which to attempt an assessment of the present situation
of Catholics in England and Wales in terms of their relationship to
their social environment. In his study of the Jewish minority in
Britain, Freedman puts forward the theory that Jews in Britain
have set out to become assimilated with the host society.[3] They
have achieved a degree of assimilation by making considerable
concessions to their environment and have shed national customs
and language. In order, however, to avoid losing their identity
altogether and becoming submerged completely the Jews have
retained their religion. This gives them an identity within society;
a means by which they can recognise each other and by which
society can recognise them.

Herberg, describing the process of assimilation of immigrant
groups in America, develops a theory along similar lines.[4] According to this an immigrant group settles into the host society by

---

[1] See Townsend, *op. cit.*
[2] See Liepmann, Kate K. *The Journey to Work* (London, 1944).
[3] Freedman, M. *A Minority in Britain* (London). *op. cit.*
[4] Herberg, W. *Protestant, Catholic, Jew* (Doubleday, 1955), *op. cit.* See also
Robbins, R. 'American Jews and American Catholics: Two types of Social
Change' (*Sociological Analysis*, vol. 26, no. 1, 1965).

abandoning the habits and customs of the country of its origin; it must do this in order to get rid of the outward marks of difference between itself and its new environment. But some characteristic feature of the group must be retained in order to give its members some identity in the larger society, and the feature that is retained is religion. As a result, a completely Americanised group emerges, fully identified with the American culture but achieving this identity through membership of a particular religious community. To quote Herberg himself . . .

'For the third generation, the American-born children of the American-born or bred children of immigrants, American reality has taken on another aspect. . . . They realise that integration into American life implies assimilation to the American model in many crucial respects. . . . The newcomer is expected to change many things about him as he becomes American—nationality, language, culture. One thing, however, he is *not* expected to change—and that is his religion. And so it is religion that with the third generation has become the differentiating element and the context of self-identification and social location.'[1]

Another American sociologist, J. L. Thomas, in his examination of the dilemmas of Irish Catholics in America, indicates that the main problem confronting the Irish immigrants was how to maintain their religion intact while at the same time achieving some measure of integration with the host society.[2] The solution was found in a historical process which involved, at first, the formation of group solidarity; this 'solidarity' allowed a bridging of the gap between each generation so that the old ideology, based on religion, could be maintained at the same time as new customs and practices, congenial to the new environment are introduced.

From these analyses it is possible to construct a process of assimilation which goes through three stages. There is first the stage of isolation which occurs when the first immigrants enter

---

[1] Herberg, *op. cit.*, p. 35. See also Stein, M. R. *The Eclipse of Community* (Princeton, 1960).

[2] Thomas, J. L. *The American Catholic Family* (New York, 1956).

the new society. They feel themselves 'different' from everybody else, they possess customs and traditions and a religion which mark them out as strangers, and their initial reaction is to withdraw in self-defence from contact with outsiders. A second stage follows when this defensive isolation is being broken down and the old traditions are being replaced by those common to the larger society in which the group is situated. This is followed by the third stage in which the descendants of the immigrants become assimilated with their environment, retaining only one feature of their origin— in this case religion—to serve as a means of identity and 'social location'.[1]

If this theory of a process of assimilation through stages is applied to urban Catholics in England and Wales then some key to explaining the present situation of these Catholics is provided. There was, to begin with, the formation of the 'closed group' of Catholics in the towns, with contact with the outside world reduced to a minimum and with the development of an institutionalised community life. This enabled the Catholic to live a sheltered existence in a different world almost from his fellow men. He had to venture from it, it is true, to earn his bread and butter but he could, if he chose, satisfy all his other needs as a social being within its confines. His education he could get in his parish school; his recreation could be found in the 'social' activities of the parish hall and if he felt the need to express talents for organising or managing the affairs of his fellows then he need not look to 'public service' but could choose from a host of parish or diocesan organisations anxious for chairmen or secretaries or committeemen. Above all, he had a source of authority to refer to in the form of the parish priest, a benevolent father figure whose pronouncements relieved him of the responsibility of decision making.

---

[1] This does not necessarily imply that the immigrants have retained their religion *only* because it gives them a means of location in society generally. The shedding of national characteristics and the movement from a particular social status has left religion as the only feature which distinguishes them from others in society generally. Hence it is religion which gives them a social identity. It may be that there is a proportion of Catholics who retain membership of the Church only because it gives them a feeling of security, of 'belonging' to an identifiable group. But any attempt to identify such Catholics would lead into an examination of motivation which lies outside the scope of this study.

During the last twenty years, and for the reasons we have mentioned, this community life has been breaking down and the urban Catholics of England and Wales are moving into the second stage— the transition from isolation to assimilation. But at this point we must note distinct differences between the process of assimilation of Irish Catholics in America and the Jewish minority in Britain, and that of the urban Catholics in England and Wales.

The first major difference lies in the fact that America is a country that has been to a large extent built up by an immigrant population. The Irish immigrants arrived in America as part of the enormous influx of people who went there to settle in the nineteenth century. So great was the extent of immigration in the nineteenth century that by the end of this period the British-Protestant element in the U.S.A. had been reduced to less than 50 per cent of the population. The Irish were not coming to a static and stratified 'native' society but to one which was constantly changing and developing. As a result, Catholic migrants to the New World, though they shared exactly the same background as those to England, did not encounter the same social problems. Most of the other immigrants who were constituting more than half of American society had similar peasant origins to the Irish.

Furthermore, the force of successive waves of immigration to America meant that the Irish did not occupy a low social status for so long as they did in England. A pattern emerged whereby each new group which came pushed up the level of its predecessors and in turn was pushed up by its successors. This process of advancement did not take place smoothly; there was friction and conflict. But the fact that it took place at all indicates a fluidity in American society that was not present in Britain.

This 'push' towards upward mobility was reinforced by other factors. Education and acculturation to American ways provided the immigrant with a means of securing his new social position and of improving on it. In concrete terms this meant that the sons of unskilled immigrants in the labouring class were able to compete for better jobs with people who were already higher in the social scale.

At each stage of the integration process, then, there were

differences between Irish immigrants in America and in England. The first stage of isolation in America did not persist for long because of the social pressures which produced fluidity in society and because of the opportunities, through education and accultura- tion, to rise in the social scale. In England and Wales the first stage has endured for a very much longer period, one of the major factors being the lack of opportunity to move out of a low social category.

A further difference lies in the 'motive power' behind the move- ment out of isolation and towards assimilation. It is very apparent in the studies conducted in America, that the immigrant Catholics wanted to identify themselves with their environment. There is a positive desire to become 'American' and to accept as many of the standards and as much of the culture of the 'American way of life' as possible. The only problem, as Thomas points out, was how was this to be done without at the same time sacrificing their religion; and the solution has emerged whereby membership of a religious group has become a means of self-identification within a larger society.

These same considerations apply to the Jewish minority in Britain. It emerges from Freedman's study that there was a strong desire on the part of many Jews to become accepted within society as a whole, and that great importance was attached to adopting the social standards, customs and habits of the particular social class to which the individual Jew aspired. Those members of the group who achieved high social rank, particularly if it meant also gaining a title, gained great prestige amongst their co-religionists and were regarded as having brought honour to the Jewish community as a whole.[1]

This positive motive to assimilate is one feature which is con- spicuously lacking amongst immigrant Catholics in England. The whole weight of this study has indicated that urban Catholics did not want to 'become English' in the sense of adopting the standards, customs and political outlook and aspirations of the host society. As has been demonstrated, the opposite in fact was true; it was considered disloyalty to Ireland to 'become English' and dangerous to the individual's Catholic faith to come into too close contact with

[1] Cf. Freedman, *op. cit.*, part IV, 'The Jews in the Society of Britain'.

non-Catholics. Isolation, then, was not only endured but deliberately encouraged. Because of this, movement into the second stage
of assimilation has been held back so long that there has been
ample time for a tradition to be established which could make such
a movement extremely painful for individual Catholics. Membership of the Catholic Church has now become firmly established in
the minds of many Catholics as a reason for remaining as aloof as
possible from their non-Catholic fellows. The social, national and
religious factors which made for isolation have merged to produce
a mentality in which Catholics have accepted the fact of separation
from the rest of society as being an integral part of their faith as
Catholics. Church authorities have constantly encouraged this
attitude; there has been, for instance, the repeated insistence on
the vital necessity of a separate system of Catholic education *as a
means of preserving the faith of the children.* Catholic parents were
reminded of their *religious* duty to maintain this separation and,
until recently, were forbidden to send their children to state
schools when there were Catholic schools available in the area.

This pressure has been applied in spheres other than education.
There was, for instance, the common practice, persisting until very
recently, of reading a short announcement after the calling of
banns in church. This announcement began 'the Church has
always forbidden mixed marriages and considers them unlawful
and pernicious. . . .' It went on to warn Catholics to 'avoid familiar
friendships with non-Catholics of the opposite sex' and stated that
if such a friendship had been formed it was the Catholic's duty to
inform the friend of the Church's rules concerning mixed marriages.
There has also been a constant desire for the establishment of
Catholic youth clubs, with the aim of bringing young Catholics
together and so helping to minimise the possibility of later 'mixed
marriages'. It is not then surprising if Catholics regard their separation as something demanded of them by their religion; and that,
conversely, if there are signs of this separation breaking down that
they are going to be seriously worried by what appears to them to
be a denial of something integral to their religious beliefs. In this
way, a state of isolation in society, brought about by a combination
of factors some of which had nothing to do with religious belief

has been confused with being an essential prerequisite of membership of the Catholic Church. This, in turn, could lead to the
prolongation of isolation long after the physical causes—historical,
social, political—have disappeared.

Unlike their American counterparts, then, movement into the
'second stage' of assimilation is something which is not coming
from within the Catholic groups but is being forced upon them by
the operation of social factors which it is beyond their power to
control. The breaking-up of the old working-class communities
and parishes and the scattering of their members throughout the
cities, the increased opportunities for social mobility and the extension of educational facilities to the children of the poor are all
features of English urban life and Catholics have been subjected to
these pressures as well as everybody else. Whether they like it or
not, Catholics are being forced out of the old pattern of life and are
having to face the problems of re-adjustment to new styles of living
in contemporary urban society in England and Wales.

With this as a basic hypothesis it is possible to highlight some of
the areas of urban Catholic life in which future sociological enquiry
could be relevant and fruitful. The first of these is in the effects
that the change in the social position of urban Catholicism is having
on the basic unit of the Church's organisation—the parish. The
formal 'ideal' of the parish envisages the existence of a community
of people living in a strictly limited geographical area. Membership
of the parish is related only to the actual physical location of the
person concerned, and each member is expected to fulfil his
religious obligations within the framework of whatever parish he
might find himself in. He is also expected to acknowledge the
religious authority of his particular parish priest and to consider
himself subordinate to the parish clergy in functional importance,
authority, power and prestige.[1] This structure worked adequately
enough in the urban areas of England and Wales during the

---

[1] See Donovan, J. D. 'The Social Structure of the Parish' in Nuesse, C. J. and
Harte, T. J. (eds.) *The Sociology of the Parish* (Bruce, Milwaukee, 1951). There
is an extensive and growing literature on various sociological aspects of the parish,
most of it published outside England. See Bibliography, and also Carrier, H.
*The Sociology of Religious Belonging* (New York, 1965), in particular chapter 8.

nineteenth and early part of the twentieth centuries because, as has been shown, the emphasis was on the forming of a closed society with its own social institutions. The urban Catholic parishes were mainly in working-class areas where there was a geographically cohesive group of people and close family and neighbourhood ties. Successive generations of Catholics were born into the same parish, attended the parish school, left it to work in an industry located close to their homes and married and settled in the same parish. The social forces mentioned earlier as operating in the last twenty years were not exerting the same pressure then and there was not much of a shift in the parish population.

In this situation, and because of the particular social and historical factors operating, the position and authority of the parish priest became of considerable importance in spheres other than the purely spiritual. This state of affairs was not restricted entirely to England. A similar situation existed for a long time on the continent of Europe and in some of the more rural areas of Belgium, for example, it exists still. Even so there was a difference in the degree of prestige and authority which an urban parish priest enjoyed in England and Wales compared to his counterpart in other countries. The priest in England was dealing with an immigrant flock of low social status in a society largely hostile to Catholicism. Immigrant Catholics brought with them from Ireland a tradition of great respect for the clergy and this meant that they were prepared to look to the priest for leadership in their new environment. In many cases the priest was often the only person anyway who was equipped by education, experience and—to some extent—social status to take the lead in providing all the community facilities for his flock— school, church, hall, parish organisations, etc.—and to deal on their behalf with local officialdom. The net result has been twofold: there has been a complete confusion of the spheres in which a priest is entitled to and expected to exercise his authority as an ordained minister; his consent and advice is now sought in all sorts of practical matters in which he cannot possibly be qualified to make a decision and he carries the burden of knowing that his parishioner will be heavily influenced by what he has to say. A view of the parish has emerged, also, in which the community structure is seen as a pyramid with the laity grouped at the base and the priest occupying a position of unchallenged authority at the apex.

Recent research indicates that this conception of the parish as a real 'community' may have been justifiable up to the pre-war period but is not justifiable now.[1] It is apparent that while many parishioners recognise an obligation to help financially towards the upkeep of church and pastor and pay lip-service to the 'ideal' of 'parish life', only a small percentage actually see the parish as the centre of their lives. Many Catholics know their fellow-parishioners but do not count them as friends, are aware that there are fellow-Catholics running shops and businesses but do not patronise them and in general are not conscious any longer of belonging to a community'.[2]

Educational developments seem to be playing a large part in the process of disintegration of the parish. By 1939 many parishes in large cities were equipped with Catholic 'all-age' schools, i.e. schools in which all the children of the parish were educated until the age of 11, at which stage a small percentage left for the local Catholic grammar school. The remainder stayed behind in the same school until they reached the age of 14. It was thus likely that the bulk of the children would receive their entire education within the parish boundaries and under the direct influence of the parish priest. Since 1945 the position has been changing. The 1944 Education Act abolished all age schools in principle and substituted instead a tripartite system of education for those over the age of 11. At that age children were to be divided into those suitable for grammar school education, those suitable for 'technical' education and those—by far the greatest number—who showed no special aptitudes and were to be lumped altogether in what were called 'secondary modern' schools. The educational merits of this scheme are not considered here: the main point is that Catholics now had

[1] See Ward, C. K. *Priest and People: A study in the sociology of religion* (Liverpool, 1961), and 'Some aspects of the social structure of a Roman Catholic parish' (*Sociological Review*, vol. VI, 1958, pp. 75–93). Dr. Ward's researches were conducted on a parish established in an industrial town in the last quarter of the nineteenth century as a result of the influx of Irish immigrants.

[2] Ward, *op. cit.* This conclusion may be drawn from the combined weight of both Dr. Ward's studies.

to provide not one school but two—a junior school and a 'secondary modern' schools—to replace one all-age school. This was beyond the means of most parishes, both in terms of numbers of pupils to fill a second, completely separate senior school and in terms of financial resources to build it. A solution was for a number of parishes to join together to build one school in common which would take children from several different areas, and this was the practice followed by Catholics in many towns. One of the major social results has been that for the first time since an organised framework of Catholic education was established in the major towns of Britain in the nineteenth century all the children in most areas are leaving their home parishes at the age of 11 to complete their education outside it. Their sense of belonging to a single social unit is thus undermined at a very early age. This process may well be accelerated by the new patterns of secondary education which are now emerging in England and Wales and to which Catholics will have to conform if they are not to be left behind the system.

The children who go to grammar schools are also providing a problem for those concerned with maintaining the old ideal of the parish. A recent investigation in a large industrial city in the north of England has indicated that those pupils who stay on at Catholic grammar schools to the age of 18 find that in many ways the milieu of the parish is no longer congenial to them.[1] Their standard of education has given them wider interests and an outlook on life which makes it impossible for them to slip snugly back into some parochial niche. They retain respect for the parochial clergy as ordained ministers but they are not prepared to accept the priest's authority in as wide a sphere as were their less well-educated counterparts. Some of the clergy themselves remarked on this and a number of them deplored the change in relationships which had taken place.[2]

Whether it is deplorable or not, the fact remains that social changes are bringing such pressures to bear upon the parish that

[1] See Brothers, J. B. *Church and School: A Study of the Impact of Education on Religion* (Liverpool, 1964).
[2] See Brothers, J. B. 'Social change and the role of the priest' (*Social Compass*, vol. X, no. 6, 1963).

its whole existence as a unit is being called into question. The problem has become obvious to some members of the Catholic Church and there is growing discussion in certain circles about the future of the parish.[1] Even so, most of this debate seems to start from the assumption that what is needed are modifications and adjustments to the existing structure in order to ease the difficulties brought about by change. There seems to be very little thought given to the idea that the whole concept of the parish is based on an idea of 'community' which may no longer be relevant to contemporary urban society.

This lack is constantly being demonstrated, particularly in discussions about experiments in the parish. One recent example will help to illustrate this. In one of its issues of June 1966 a Catholic weekly newspaper gave a lengthy account of the difficulties being experienced in Islington, a parish in London, and the attempts that were being made to overcome them. The article begins by asking the question 'How can a parish be effective in an urbanised society where 99 per cent of the population are perfect strangers?' and goes on to state that 'The congregation is a "family" no longer and the problem is worsening as the mobility of the nation's labour force increases. In suburbia, in the new housing estates, and in the older established communities parish priests face the problem of unifying people who sometimes through apathy and complacency are reluctant to be brought together.' The parish at Islington contained 'bus-conductors, labourers, stockbrokers and solicitors'—in other words it was almost a cross-section of society generally—and in the words of the parish priest 'The problems of welding such diverse backgrounds and minds into a community are immense.'

The point to note is that the basic assumption behind the article —and behind the activities of the priests mentioned—is that a geographical area which is given the name 'parish' can and must in some way be made into a 'community'. Parish priests are said to be confronted with the task of 'unifying people' and if such a task proves difficult then it must be at least partly because people are

[1] See, for example, Davis *et al.*, *The Parish in the Modern World* (London, 1965).

'reluctant' to be so unified as a result of their 'apathy and complacency'. It is implicitly believed that ways and means can be found to 'unite' people who happen to live within certain physical boundaries so that they form a 'real community'; and when there is talk of 'change' and 'experiment' in connection with the parish, it is change and experiment with these ways and means that is meant and not with the concept of 'parish' itself. The parish priest at Islington, after making valiant efforts, confessed that 'so far success has been minimal', and that he felt that 'on the sociological front the Church has very little influence'. It may perhaps make his task, and those of many other priests, easier in the future if the whole basic approach to the problem of 'community' were changed. Instead of trying to mould an artificial unity it may be more fruitful to enquire first into the formal and informal links—based on family, professional and social interests—which actually do bring people together in groups within society generally, and to try to build a community built on a real association.

Important features in the life of Catholics in England are the various associations and societies for lay people which exist. These can be at parochial or diocesan level—like the Union of Catholic Mothers, the St. Vincent de Paul Society, the Knights of St. Columba—with a national body providing some co-ordination of their activities, or they can be linked with professional or occupational status—like the Union of Catholic Students, the Newman Association (primarily for university graduates), the Guild of SS. Luke, Cosmos and Damian (for Catholic doctors) and the Catenian Association (for Catholic business and professional men generally), which are organised at national level and have local branches all over the country. These organisations, comprising, as they do, a hard core of 'active' Catholics in every field, could play a very important part in deciding both the future rate of the process of assimilation of Catholics into English society and the direction that that process could take. Much will depend on the motives of the individual Catholics who join these associations and share in directing their policies, and here another sphere of research is opened up. Are people attracted to joining these groups because they see in them a means of redirecting their close social contacts to Catholics; because, in other words, they wish to re-create in another form the 'closed community' which is now disappearing? If this is the case then the existence of the organisation will act as an impediment to assimilation.

Often the reason given for membership of any of these groups is purely religious, i.e. that they provide an extension and continuation of education in the Catholic Faith and hence prepare their members not only to live better lives as Christians but also to be active in 'Christianising' their environment. The validity of this high motive is not in question; what is important, however, is the effect that this reasoning has upon the attitude of the Catholic member of one of these groups to his social environment generally. Does he regard his group as providing a position of strength from which to launch a 'Catholic attack' on society, or does he regard it as a means of preparing him as a Christian to take an equal share with his fellow-citizens in creating a 'good society'? Both of these attitudes will obviously have an effect upon the process of assimilation. The implications of the second do not need to be elaborated but the point may be made, in connection with the first attitude—of regarding the Catholic society as a 'strongpoint'—that it can produce a hostile reaction amongst non-Catholics who may regard such associations as 'pressure groups' aimed at benefiting Catholics at the expense of everyone else.[1]

There are other forms of association which could play an important part in the process of assimilation. There have always existed formal groups of Catholics who join together for purely social reasons: the working-class parishes for instance had their 'clubs', restricted to men and equipped with bars and the usual trappings of a working man's club. It might be expected that the popularity of these will decrease if only because of the loss of population from the old areas and the difficulty of finding premises—and support—in the new suburban areas. There are signs, however, that these Catholic 'social' institutions are being replaced by associations more suited by their nature to the new prosperity and class location of the urban Catholics. Hence there are now, in some areas,

[1] Cf. Goddijn, W. 'Catholic minorities and social integration' (*Social Compass*, vol. VII, no. 1–2, 1960).

Catholic tennis clubs, and 'dining-out' groups are making their appearance among the social activities of some of the local circles of the Newman Association. The continuance of this trend in the future may indicate that Catholics are attempting to reconstruct their separate community life in a way that is more pertinent to the changed social conditions;[1] this indicating, in its turn, that 'exclusiveness' will continue to survive the demise of the particular circumstances that brought it about and that many Catholics will remain lacking in any positive desire to assimilate with their fellow-citizens.

One final, and extremely important area of research remains to be mentioned. Discussion so far has been of the position of the Catholic laity in England and Wales; there remains to be considered the position of the priest. It has already been shown that circumstances helped to bring about a considerable amount of confusion concerning the status and function of the clergy—particularly the parish priest—and that the spheres of priestly authority had been extended to include other than the purely spiritual. Now that conditions have changed so that the priest is no longer the 'natural' leader he once was, has no longer a fairly static and socially 'immobile' group of parishioners to deal with and has, indeed, to minister to a growing group of Catholics whose education is often superior to his own and who are sometimes capable—and eager—to dispute with him in matters of theology, it appears necessary to re-define his role in society. Basic research has already been started by sociologists in Europe, North America and Latin America but it will not be sufficient to import their

[1] Cf. Greeley, A. M. 'Interaction between religious groups in an upper middle class Roman Catholic parish' (*Social Compass*, vol. IX, no. 1–2, 1962). Much of this particular issue of *Social Compass* was devoted to a sociological phenomenon defined as 'vertical pluralism', *i.e.* that, in a community containing both Catholics and Protestants of a similar social standing, each group will either develop its own social institutions, which are exclusively Catholic or exclusively Protestant, or, if they share a common institution (*e.g.* a golf or tennis club), then that institution will be rigidly divided into a Catholic and a Protestant section.

Dr. Greeley pointed out in his article (on an American suburban parish) that such a division was evident on the golf course—'it was a rare foursome which contained members of both groups'—at dances, where there was no dancing with members of the other group, and that it even intruded into adult parties where 'the two groups stayed on opposite sides of the room'.

conclusions—when they have made them—wholesale and apply them to England and Wales.[1] The position of the priest in relation to the laity varies, naturally, from society to society and from epoch to epoch, and the course of the development of urban Catholicism in England and Wales from the start of the nineteenth century to the present time is not paralleled in any country in Europe or North America. Any such research conducted by sociologists would need to be done with constant reference to experts in other disciplines— theology, history and psychology in particular—but the need for a re-definition of priestly roles and the development of a sociology of the priesthood is becoming very apparent in England, as everywhere else.

[1] The 'pioneer' work in this field was done by Professor John D. Donovan of Boston College, U.S.A., in his Ph.D. thesis on 'The Catholic Priest: A study in the Sociology of the Professions' (unpublished Ph.D. thesis, Harvard, 1951).

Since then a number of works have appeared (see Bibliography) and at the present time (February 1966) active research is being conducted on the 'public image' of the priest by the centres of socio-religious research at Lille, France, and Santiago di Chile, South America. Also, Professor Donovan, who has recently spent a sabbatical year as visiting professor at the University of Louvain, Belgium, is working on a study provisionally entitled 'Towards a Sociology of the Priesthood'.

# Sources

*The Tablet*
*The Cambrian*
*The Merlin*
*The Political Register*
*The Cardiff and Merthyr Guardian*
*The Laity's Directory*
*Ordo*

Francis, J.   *A Sermon to the working Classes preached in St. Paul's Church, Newport.* 21 April 1839 (Newport: The Public Library). The 'Advertisement' to the second edition of this sermon published 6 November 1839 (Newport: The Public Library).

Taylor, J. R.   *A Sermon on the late Chartist insurrection, preached at the St. Woollos Church,* 16 November 1839 (Newport: The Public Library).

*Report to the General Board of Health on a Preliminary Inquiry into the Sewerage, Drainage, and Supply of Water, and the Sanitary Condition of the Inhabitants of the Borough of Preston,* George Thomas Clark, London, 1849.

*Report to the General Board of Health on a Preliminary Inquiry into the Sewerage, Drainage, and Supply of Water, and the Sanitary Condition of the Inhabitants of the Borough of Birmingham,* London, 1849.

*Report to the General Board of Health on a Preliminary Inquiry into the Sewerage, Drainage, and Supply of Water, and the Sanitary Condition of the Inhabitants, of the Borough of Manchester,* London, 1849.

*Report to the General Board of Health on a Preliminary Inquiry into the Sewerage, Drainage, and Supply of Water, and the Sanitary Condition of the Inhabitants, of the Borough of Cardiff,* London, 1850.

*Report to the General Board of Health on a Preliminary Inquiry into the Sewerage, Drainage, and Supply of Water, and the Sanitary Condition of the Inhabitants, of the Borough of Merthyr,* London, 1850.

Reports of the medical officer of health, *Liverpool,* 1847–50.

Reports of the medical officer of health, *Cardiff,* 1863–88.

*Second Report of the Central Board of His Majesty's Commissioners for inquiring into the Employment of Children in Factories,* 1833.

*Report of the Select Committee on Poor Removal,* 1854.

*Report of the Select Committee on Poor Removal, 1855.*
*Report of the Select Committee on the State of the Poor in Ireland, 1830.*
*Report of the Poor Law Commissioners, 1834.*
*First Report from His Majesty's Commissioners for inquiring into the condition of the Poorer Classes in Ireland, 1835.* See appendices 'A' and 'G' of the above Report; latter dealing with the condition of the Irish poor in Britain.
*Report of the Commission on Emigration and Other Population Problems.* Dublin, 1952.
*Report of the Commission on the State of Education in Wales,* 1847.
*Census of Great Britain,* 1811.
*Censuses of Great Britain,* 1851–1951.
The Cardiff Diary of the Fathers of the Institute of Charity (see Cronin, J. M. below).
The Log-Book of the Parish of St Mary of the Angels, Cardiff.
Marriage and Burial Registers of the Parish Church of St John, Cardiff.
National Library of Wales, ms. 4378, pp. 86–7.
Collected unpublished papers of Rev. J. M. Cronin, Institute of Charity, County Record Office, Cardiff. This collection includes a typescript of parts of the Cardiff Diary of the Fathers of the Institute of Charity. The original of this document was not available for consultation.
*Cardiff Records* (Cardiff Public Library, vols. I–VI).
*Irish Trade Journal and Statistical Bulletin. 1955* (Central Statistics Office, Dublin).
*Cardiff Archdiocesan Year Book, 1956.*
*St Peter's Magazine,* 1920–29. Issued monthly during these years.

# Bibliography

Albion, G., 'The Restoration of the Hierarchy' (in Beck, ed., *op. cit.*).
Anson, P. F., *The Religious Orders and Congregations of Great Britain and Ireland* (London, 1949).
Ashton, T. S., *The Industrial Revolution in the Eighteenth Century* (London, 1955).
Beales, A. C. F., 'The Struggle for the Schools' (in Beck, ed., *op. cit.*).
— 'Beginnings of Catholic Elementary Education in the Second Spring', *Dublin Review*, October 1939.
— 'Religious Education in England, Past, Present and Future', *Sword of the Spirit*, 1944.
— 'Some Delusions of Catholic Education' (*Bradford C.P.E.A.*, 1944).
— 'Catholic Education in England', *Lumen Vitae*, Louvain, vol. 1, no. 3, 1946.
— 'The Free Churches and the Catholic Schools', *The Month*, November–December 1943.
— 'The Catholic Schools Crisis of 1950', *Catholic Social Guild*, 1950.
Banton, M., *The Coloured Quarter* (London, 1955).
Battersby, W. J., 'Secondary Education for Boys' (in Beck, ed., *op. cit.*).
— 'Educational Work of the Religious Orders of Women' (in Beck, ed., *op. cit.*).
Beck, G. (ed.), *The English Catholics, 1850–1950*, (London 1950).
Benedict, R., *Patterns of Culture* (New York, 1934).
Bentwich, N., *The Jews in our Time* (London, Pelican Books, 1960).
Bogan, B., 'The Irish in Southwark', *Christus Rex*, vol. 12, no. 1.
Bott, E., *Family and Social Network* (London).
Bottomore, T., 'Social Stratification in Voluntary Organisations' (in Glass, ed., *op. cit.*, pp. 349–82).
Boulard, F., *An Introduction to Religious Sociology* (London, 1960).
Bray, R. A., *Labour and the Churches* (London, 1912).
Briggs, A. (ed.), *Chartist Studies* (London, 1959).
Brothers, J., *Church and School* (Liverpool, 1964).
— 'Social Change and the Role of the Priest', *Social Compass*, vol. X/6, 1963.
Brown, J. A. C., *The Social Psychology of Industry* (London, 1954).

Butler, E. C., *Life and Times of Bishop Ullathorne, 1806–1888* (London, 1926).

Calley, M. J. C., *God's People. West Indian Pentecostal Sects in England* (London, 1965).

Carrier, H., *The Sociology of Religious Belonging* (New York, 1965).

Carter and Downham, *The Communication of Ideas* (London, 1954).

Charlton, B., *Recollections of a Northumbrian Lady* (London, 1949).

Church, R., *The Oxford Movement, 1833–1845* (London, 1891).

Clapham, J. H., *An Economic History of Modern Britain* (Cambridge, 1926).

Cole, G. D. H., *Studies in Class Structure* (London, 1955).

Collins, S., *Coloured Minorities in Britain* (London, 1957).

Connolly, J., *Labour, Nationality and Religion* (in Reynolds and Taylor, *op. cit.*).

Coulson, Allchin and Trevor, *Newman: A Portrait Restored* (London, 1965).

Cronin, J. M., *Catholic Cardiff: Past and Present* (Cardiff, 1922).

— *Ireland and Wales: Early bounds of kinship* (Cardiff, 1925).

Cunningham, A., *et al, Catholics and the Left* (London, 1966).

Curtis, E., *A History of Ireland* (London, 1936).

Davis and others. *The Parish in the Modern World* (London, 1965).

De Beaumont, G., *Ireland; Social, Political and Religious* (London, 1839).

De Vries, E., *Man in Rapid Social Change* (S.C.M. Press, 1961).

Dennis, Henriques and Slaughter, *Coal is our Life* (London, 1956).

Dillon, P., 'The Irish in Chicago', *Christus Rex*, vol. 12, no. 1.

Donovan, J., *The Academic Man in the Catholic College* (New York, 1964).

— 'The Social Structure of the Parish' (in Neusse and Harte, eds., *op. cit.*).

— Catholic Priests: A Study in the Sociology of the Professions (unpubl. Ph.D. thesis, Harvard, 1951).

Dunlop, R., *Life of Daniel O'Connell* (1900).

Durkheim, E., *The Elementary Forms of the Religious Life* (New York Free Press edn., 1965).

Eagleton, T., 'Priests and Paternalism', *New Blackfriars*, December 1965.

Engels, F., *The Condition of the Working Class in England in 1844* (London, 1888).

Ensor, R. C. K., *England, 1870–1914* (Oxford, 1936).

Evans, E. W., *The Miners of South Wales* (Cardiff, 1961).

/Evennett, H. O., 'Catholics and the Universities' (in Beck, ed., *op. cit.*).

— *The Catholic Schools of England* (Cambridge, 1944).

Faulkner, H. U., 'Chartism and the Churches' (in Rosenblatt, *op. cit.*).

Fichter, J., *Southern Parish, I*, Dynamics of a City Church, Chicago, 1951).
— 'Social Relations in the Urban Parish' (Chicago, 1954).
— 'The Parish and Social Integration', *Social Compass*, no. 1, 1960.
Fitzsimons, J. (ed.), *Manning: Anglican and Catholic* (London, 1951).
Fogarty, M. P., *Christian Democracy in Western Europe, 1820–1953* (London, 1957).
Frazier, E. F., *The Negro Church in America* (Liverpool University Press, 1964).
Freedman, M., *A Minority in Britain* (London, 1957).
Gammage, R. G., *History of the Chartist Movement* (see Halévy, *op. cit.*).
Ginsberg, M., *The Psychology of Society* (University Paperbacks, London, 1964).
Glass, D. V. (ed.), *Social Mobility in Britain* (London, 1954).
Glock, C. Y., 'The Role of Deprivation in the Origin and Evolution of Religious Groups' (in Lee and Marty, eds., *op. cit.*).
Goddijn, W., 'Catholic Minorities and Social Integratin', *Socialo Compass*, vol. VII, no. 2, 1960.
Greeley, A. M., 'Interaction between religious groups in an upper middle class Roman Catholic parish', *Social Compass*, vol. IX/1–2, 1962.
— *Religion and Career: A study of college graduates* (New York, 1963).
Gwynn, D., *The English Catholics, 1850–1950* (London, 1950).
Halévy, E., *A History of the English People in the Nineteenth Century* (London, 1948–50).
Halmos, P., *Towards a Measure of Man* (London, 1957).
— *Solitude and Privacy: A study of social isolation* (London, 1952).
Hammond, J. L. and B., *The Age of the Chartists* (London, 1930).
— *The Village Labourer* (London, 1949).
— *The Town Labourer* (London, 1949).
— *The Bleak Age* (London, 19  ).
Herberg, W., *Protestant, Catholic, Jew* (New York, 1955).
— 'Religious Group Conflict in America' (in Lee and Marty, eds., *op. cit.*).
Hobsbawn, E., *Working Man: Studies in the History of Labour* (London, 1965).
Houtart, F., *Les paroisses de Bruxelles, 1803–1951* (Louvain, 1954).
Hughes, P., 'The Coming Century' (in Beck, ed., *op. cit.*).
— 'The English Catholics in 1850' (in Beck, ed., *op. cit.*).
Inglis, K. S., *Churches and the Working Classes in Victorian England* (London, 1963).
Jenkins, J. A. and James, R. E., *The History of Nonconformity in Cardiff* (Cardiff, 1901).

Jenkins, R. T., *Hanes Cymru yn y Ddeunawfed Gantif* (Cardiff, 1931).

John, A. H., *The Industrial Development of South Wales* (University of Wales Press, 1950).

Johnson, H., *Sociology* (London, 1961).

Johnson, H. J., 'Cardinal Newman' (in Beck, ed., *op. cit.*).

Lee, R. and Marty, M. (eds.), *Religion and Social Conflict* (New York, 1964).

Lewis, J. P., 'The Anglicisation of Glamorgan', *Transactions of the Glamorgan Local History Society, vol. IV, 1960*.

Lewis, R. and Maude, A., *The English Middle Classes* (London, Pelican Books, 1953).

Leys, Mary, *Catholics in England, 1559–1829* (London, 1961).

Liepmann, K., *The Journey to Work* (London, 1944).

Lipset, S. M., 'Religion and Politics in the American Past and Present' (in Lee and Marty, eds., *op. cit.*).

Little, K., *Negroes in Britain* (London, 1948).

Lloyd, M. G. and Thomason, G. F., *Welsh Society in Transition*. A Survey of Recent Researches into the Social Structure of Wales (Cardiff, 1963).

Lovett, W., *My Life and Struggles* (see Halévy, *op. cit.*).

Mann, H., *Religious Worship in England and Wales* (London, 1854).

Mantoux, P., *The Industrial Revolution in the Eighteenth Century* (London, 1955).

Mannheim, K., *Diagnosis of Our Time* (London, 1943).

Marsh, D. C., *The Changing Social Structure of England and Wales, 1871–1951* (London, 1958).

Marshall, D., *English People in the Eighteenth century* (London, 1956).

Mastermann, C. F. G., *The Condition of England* (London, 1909).

Mathew, D., *Catholicism in England, 1535–1935* (London, 1936).

— 'Old Catholics and Converts' (in Beck, ed., *op. cit.*).

Matthijssen, M., 'Catholic intellectual emancipation in the Western Countries of mixed religion', *Social Compass*, vol. VI, 1958–9.

Maxwell, C., *Country and Town in Ireland under the Georges* (London, 1940).

McClelland, V. A., *Cardinal Manning: His Public Life and Influence, 1865–92* (London, 1962).

McCord, N., *The Anti-Corn Law League* (London, 1958).

Moberg, D., 'Religion and Society in the Netherlands and America', *Social Compass*, vol. IX/1–2, 1962.

Morgan, K. O., 'Democratic Politics in Glamorgan, 1884–1914', *Transactions of the Glamorgan Local History Society*, vol. IV, 1960.

Mudie-Smith, R., *The Religious Life of London* (London, 1904).

Newman, J. H., *Apologia Pro Vita Sua* (London, 1864).

— *Present Position of Catholics in England* (London, 1851).

— *The Second Spring*, sermon preached at the first provincial synod of Westminster, Oscott, 1852.

Nuesse, C. J. and Harte, T. J., *The Sociology of the Parish* (Bruce, Milwaukee, 1951).

O'Brien, G., *Economic History of Ireland from the Union to the Famine* (London, 1921).

O'Danachair, C., 'The Family in Irish Tradition', *Christus Rex*, vol. XV, no. 3.

O'Dea, T. F., *American Catholic Dilemma* (New York, 1958).

Payne, E. A., *The Free Church Tradition in the Life of England* (London, 1951, revised edition).

Pin, E., 'Can the Urban Parish be a Community?', *Social Compass*, vol. VII, pp. 39–47.

Purcell, E. S., *Life of Cardinal Manning* (London, 1896).

Read, J. C., *The Church in Our City* (Cardiff, 1954).

Redford, A., *Labour Migration in England, 1800–1850* (Manchester, 1926).

Rees, A. D., *Life in a Welsh Countryside* (Cardiff, 1950).

Reynolds and Taylor, *British Pamphleteers*, vol. II (London, 1959).

Richmond, A. H., *The Colour Problem* (Penguin Books, 1955).

Robbins, R., 'American Jews and American Catholics: Two Types of Social Change', *Sociological Analysis*, vol. 26, no. 1, 1965.

Robertson, H. M., *Aspects of the Rise of Economic Individualism* (Cambridge, 1933).

Rosenblatt, F. F., *The Social and Economic Aspects of the Chartist Movement*, (New York, 1916).

Smelser, N. J., *Social Change in the Industrial Revolution* (London, 1959).

Snead-Cox, J. G., *Life of Cardinal Vaughan* (London, 1910).

Spencer, A. E. C. W., 'The Demography and Sociography of the Catholic Community of England and Wales', unpublished paper, 1965 (Downside Symposium).

Stein, M. R., *The Eclipse of Community* (Princeton, 1960).

Tawney, R. H., *Religion and the Rise of Capitalism* (London, Penguin Books, 1948).

Thomas, B., 'The Migration of Labour into the Glamorgan Coalfield (1861–1911)', *Economica*, 1930.

Thomas, J. L., *The American Catholic Family* (New York, 1956).

Thomason, G. F., 'The Effects of Industrial Changes on Selected Communities in South Wales' (unpublished Ph.D. Thesis, University of Wales, Cardiff, 1963).

Thompson, E. P., *The Making of the English Working Class* (London, 1963).

Townsend, P., *The Family Life of Old People* (London, 1957).

Tracy, E. J., 'American Catholics and the Intellectual Life' in Putz, L. J., ed., *The Catholic Church, U.S.A.* (Chicago, 1956).

Tressall, R., *The Ragged Trousered Philanthropists* (London, 1914).

Trevor, Meriol, *Newman: The Pillar of the Cloud* (London, 1961).

— *Newman: Light in Winter* (London, 1962).

Wach, J., *Sociology of Religion* (London, 1947).

— *The Comparative Study of Religions* (New York, 1958).

Ward, B., *The Sequel to Catholic Emancipation* (London, 1915).

Ward, C. K., *Priests and People* (Liverpool, 1961).

— 'Some Aspects of the Social Structure of a Roman Catholic Parish', *The Sociological Review*, July 1958.

Ward, W., *Life of John Henry Cardinal Newman* (London, 1912).

Weber, M., *The Protestant Ethic and the Spirit of Capitalism* (London, 1930).

— *The Sociology of Religion* (Boston, 1963).

Wickham, E. R., *Church and People in an Industrial City* (London, 1957).

Williams, D., *John Frost: a Study in Chartism* (Cardiff, 1939).

Williams, W., *The Sociology of an English Village: Gosforth* (London, 1956).

Wilson, A., *Life of Bishop Hedley* (London, 1930).

Wilson, B. R., *Sects and Society* (London, 1961).

— *Social Aspects of Religious Sects* (University of London, 1955).

Yinger, J. M., *Religion, Society and the Individual* (New York, 1957).

— *Sociology looks at Religion* (New York, 1961).

Young and Ashton, *British Social Work in the Nineteenth Century* (London, 1956).

Zweig, F., *The British Worker* (London, 1952).

— *Neighbourhood and Community* (Liverpool, 1954).

# Index

1. Nicolas Bardos-Feltoronyi: Diffusion du progrès et convergence des
   prix (Allemagne-Angleterre 1792–1913), Louvain, Editions
   Nauwelaerts, Paris, Béatrice Nauwelaerts, 1966. Un vol. in-8°
   de 230 p.
2. Georges Szapary: Diffusion du progrès et convergence des prix
   (Europe-Etats-Unis 1899–1962), Louvain, Editions Nauwelaerts,
   Paris, Béatrice Nauwelaerts, 1966. Un vol. in-8° de 246 p.
3. Herman Deleeck: Maatschappelijke zekerheid en inkomensher-
   verdeling (1948–62), Antwerpen, De Standaard, 1966.
4. Marcel van Acoleyen: Bedrijfsekonomische aspekten van de
   produktiviteitsanalyse, Antwerpen, De Standaard, 1966.
5. Florian de Vylder: Processus de Poisson généralisés. Louvain,
   Librairie universitaire, 1966. Un vol. in-8° de 187 p.
6. Karel Dobbelaere: Sociologische analyse van de katholiciteit,
   Antwerpen, De Standaard, 1966.
7. Jean Remy: La ville, phénomène économique, Bruxelles, Editions
   Vie Ouvrière, 1966.
8. J. Alberto Prades: La sociologie de la religion chez Max Weber,
   essai d'analyse et de critique de la méthode. Louvain, Editions
   Nauwelaerts, 1966.
9. A. Romaniuk: Les comportements procréatifs des populations au
   Congo.
10. Sabah el-Din el-Bakjaji: Processus stochastiques, Processus de
    Markov, Processus de renouvellement—Etude de la stabilité
    financière des caisses de Pension. Imprimerie Ceuterick, Louvain,
    1966.
11. A. R. Buzzi: La théorie politique d'Antonio Gramsci, Louvain,
    Editions Nauwelaerts, 1967.
12. Henry De Decker: Développement communautaire, une stratégie
    d'édification de la Nation. Analyse des modèles de développement
    communautaire en Guinée et au Sénégal. Kinshasa, Editions de
    l'Ires, Lovanium, Paris, Mouton et Cie, 1967.
13. Olivier Vanneste:
14. John Hickey: Urban Catholicism in England and Wales. 1829 to the
    Present Day. London, Geoffrey Chapman Ltd., 1967.